A Breeder's Companion

Record Keeping for Your Dogs' Litters

Puppies are a gift from above, entrusted to us like
precious seeds. We water them with praise, patience,
and love, and watch them grow into full bloom.

—Leila Grandemange

A Breeder's Companion • Record Keeping for Your Dogs' Litters

copyright © 2015 Leila Grandemange

first printing May, 2015

ISBN 978-0-9826854-5-7

Sunny Ville
PUBLISHING

TABLE OF CONTENTS

DISCLAIMER

THE AUTHOR IS NOT A VET. Please consult your veterinarian with questions on how to interpret any information in this book.

The publisher and author are not responsible nor liable for any veterinary medical advice, course of treatment, diagnosis, or any other information obtained from this book. Do not give medications or supplements without approval of a licensed veterinarian.

RECIPE FOR A SUCCESSFUL BREEDING PROGRAM

There are Four Essential Ingredients for a Successful Breeding Program: a good heart; a curious and creative mind; passion, patience, dedication; and lots of love!

🐾 **A Good Heart** is without a doubt one of the most important ingredients and inevitably guides all that we do. Compassionate and kind, responsible, honest, humble, and generous are all adjectives that would describe a good hearted person. I believe that a successful breeder is continually seeking these qualities and growing in them, for the betterment of humanity, and our beloved dogs. Sound, happy animals that receive good nutrition, veterinary care, time for exercise and play, and lots of TLC all reveal a masterpiece in the making!

🐾 **A Curious and Creative Mind** is another important ingredient without which the recipe will surely be bland. Learning is a life-long process and the desire for continuing education will help propel a person from average to great. So why strive for greatness and seek to master the art of breeding? Simply because our dogs deserve it! There are far too many unwanted dogs to add to the heartache. Study your breed standard, seek a mentor, become involved in dog clubs, attend dog events, and read all you can. The curious and creative mind is always asking, seeking, and stirring the pot in order to uncover new and better ways of doing things. When a problem arises it becomes part of the solution. These are the minds that strive for excellence, ensuring that they honor the legacy of those who've gone before.

🐾 **Passion, Patience, and Dedication** are crucial ingredients that often determine whether the recipe will withstand the heat. Breeding better dogs is a life-long pursuit that I would compare to a marathon rather than a quick sprint to success, and it's definitely not for the faint of heart. Qualities such as passion, patience, and dedication all play a vital role in creating a successful breeding program. "Patience" however is often the hardest to acquire. Will we be like the rabbit, in the story of "The Rabbit and the Turtle," dashing off the starting blocks full of pride, energy, and zeal, yet quickly running out of steam, hot, tired, and wanting to stop? Or will we be like the turtle who kept walking, slow and steady, step by step, carefully pacing himself, and never quitting no matter how tired he got? How dedicated are we to the journey, to our goals and dreams, and to our dogs? Do we consider their welfare above other commitments, whether personal, financial, or competitive? If we have the best breeding program in the world and our own dogs are not happy, have we truly succeeded as breeders?

🐾 **A Whole Lot of Love!** Breeding better dogs is essentially a labor of love. It's the gentle hand that mixes the ingredients and the watchful eye that oversees the details. It's the mind that recalls the wagging tails and the unconditional love that welcome us home. It's the warm feeling when goals are achieved, and the grateful heart towards those who've spurred us on. It's the awestruck wonder at the sight of a newborn litter and the lifetime commitment to each precious pup. It's the knowledge that "success" is not defined by ribbons and fame, rather by the glimmer of joy in our dogs' eyes and the companionship they share. Most importantly, it's knowing that our labor was not in vain, and that we have contributed to the wonderful world of dogs! That is the reward. That is success!

> A righteous man cares for the needs of his animal.
> —Proverbs 12:10

THE IMPORTANCE OF KEEPING RECORDS

Staying organized is an important part of being a responsible dog breeder. Strong, detailed note keeping of sire and dam, health testing completed, and litters whelped gives us valuable information which we can consult at a moment's notice. Another important reason to keep records of our dogs and litters is that it is an AKC requirement. This book was designed with that in mind. The following information on this page was prepared by and reprinted with the permission of the American Kennel Club.

Each person or firm who owns, breeds, or sells dogs that are AKC-registrable must keep accurate, up-to-date records of all transactions involving these dogs. There must be no doubt as to the identity of any individual dog or as to the parentage of a particular dog or litter.

The AKC recommends common-sense practices for those who regularly have multiple dogs or litters on their premises, including:

Permanent identification of each dog, with tattoos, microchips, marking, or tagging.

Isolation of bitches in season.

Segregation of litters whelped near the same date.

The AKC requires the owner of an AKC-registered dog to maintain the following information:

Breed

Registered name and number (or litter number if not registered)

Sex, color and markings

Date of birth

Names and numbers of sire and dam

Name of breeder

Name and address of person from whom directly acquired

Date of acquisition

Date and duration of lease, if any

The owner of a dog which is bred must record:

Date and place of mating

Names of persons handling mating

Registered name and number of dog to which mated

Name and address of its owner

The owner of a litter must record:

Date of whelping

Number of puppies whelped by sex and by color and markings

Litter registration number

Date of sale, gift or death of each puppy so described

Name and address of person acquiring each puppy so described

Kinds of papers and date supplied

Registered name and number of each puppy registered by breeder

WHELPING EQUIPMENT CHECKLIST

Have all whelping items ready and tools disinfected at least a week prior to due date.

- Your veterinarian's phone number, emergency vet number, and pet sitter/family/friend numbers in case of emergency
- Pen, paper, and a good book on whelping
- Whelping box, and a "ready box" with heat source to welcome pups as they are born
- Clean towels (preferably light in color), and wash cloths (about 2 per puppy)
- Clock and/or watch (to time births)
- Heat source (i.e. hot water bottle, snuggle safe, heating pads should never be set above low or come in direct contact with pups)
- Household thermometer (to monitor air temperature in room and whelping box)
- Thermometer (to monitor mother and pups temperature)
- K-Y Lubricating Jelly or water-based lubricant for vaginal exam if needed (never use Vaseline!)
- Paper towels, newspaper, and a large plastic bag for garbage
- Scale to weigh pups (a food scale works well)
- Sterile latex surgical gloves (keep a box of these disposable gloves handy)
- Umbilical cord care: heavy white sewing thread or unwaxed dental floss to tie the umbilical stump if needed; Q-tips, Iodine pads or liquid Betadine
- Sterile hemostat (surgical clamp) and a blunt-ended scissors to cut the cord if needed
- Isopropyl alcohol (to clean scissors and hemostat between each birth)
- Soft rubber pediatric bulb syringe or Dee Lee Mucus Trap (to clear puppies airways at birth)
- Puppy milk replacer such as Esbilac or goat's milk
- Feeding tube (size 8 french with attachable syringe, size 5 fr for pups under 8 oz), bottle and nipples (preemie size)
- Flashlight (keep bitch on leash for potty breaks after dark, with towel in hand in case she births a puppy)
- Nutri-Cal or Nutri-Drops (quick energy for mom or struggling pups)
- Electrolyte Solution or Pedialyte (for bitches drinking water or puppy hydration)
- Calsorb (a fast-absorbing oral calcium supplement to strengthen contractions if needed)
- I.D. bands for pups
- Plain cottage cheese, yogurt and/or vanilla ice cream for the bitch

Disinfecting tools: Begin by washing items in mild soap and water, rinse well. Then use boiling water (boil for 20 minutes), steam or dilute iodine, betadine, or chlorhexidine on tools. Place in a sealed container ready for use.

Recommended Resources: To learn more about the purpose and use of the items listed on the Whelping Equipment Checklist, please see page 141 for book suggestions, articles, and web links. Consult a vet if needed.

IMPORTANT
Do not give medications or supplements to your bitch or pups without approval of a veterinarian.

IMPORTANT REMINDERS

The following information is a summary of things to remember to help ensure the safe delivery of pups and the well being of the dam. It is also recommended to have a good book on whelping for more in-depth study (see Recommended Resources page 141). BE PREPARED FOR AN EMERGENCY: know where the emergency vet is located, and have your vet's phone number nearby. Prepare a "ready box" for pups with towel and heat source, and a clean crate to transport the dam to the vet if needed. Most importantly, stay close, and reassure the mother-to-be that you are there.

Gestation Period (the period from conception to birth)

- The average gestation is 63 days post ovulation (not from date of breeding). However normal gestation can be from 60-66 days. A perpetual whelping chart is located on page 17.
- A simple blood test measuring progesterone around the time of mating will help you determine a more accurate due date. Consult a vet if your bitch goes past day 63 gestation.

How to Confirm Pregnancy

- Weeks 1-2: few signs except for a slight weight gain
- Weeks 3-4: possible morning sickness (lasts only a few days), lack of appetite, vomiting on occasion
- By day 40: her belly will increase in size depending on the number of pups she is carrying. Nipples begin to enlarge
- Close to time of whelp: breasts enlarge. If expressed, a milky fluid may appear from nipples
- Palpating to feel for pups: done by vet at day 26 after last breeding
- Ultrasound of abdomen (after day 28), X-ray (after day 45 is acceptable, better on days 57-59)

Monitor and Chart Dam's Temperature Prior to Whelp (charts are found in this book)

- Starting on day 55, take dam's temperature 2-3 times daily to determine her normal temperature (a dog's normal temperature is between 100°-102.5°F). Dip the end of a rectal thermometer in K-Y Jelly to ease with insertion. To ensure accuracy, angle the thermometer to one side so it gently touches the wall of her rectum. Also, use the same thermometer each time and take it when she is calm. From day 59, you may want to add a temperature check at night.
- Approximately 24 to 48 hours prior to whelp her temperature should drop anywhere from 96°-99°F.

Signs of Impending Whelp (These are only guidelines. Some mothers-to-be give no sign. Do not leave dam unattended day or night in the week before her due date.)

- Temperature drops to 99°F or below (or 2 degrees below her normal temperature)
- Restless, digging, nesting, panting, pupils dilated, stops eating, hiding
- Looking at and licking her rear end
- Milk from nipples may appear
- Progesterone testing less than 2.5

Stages of Labor (see page 141, Recommended Resources for more in-depth explanation)

- Stage 1: dam may appear uncomfortable or restless. Lasts 6-12 hours
- Stage 2: dam may pant and lick her vulva. Involuntary uterine contractions increase which stimulate active labor. At this point she may appear anxious. After water bag breaks a pup should birth within a few minutes.
- Stage 3 labor: shortly after each puppy is born a placenta is expelled. Count the placentas and note them in the whelping chart provided in this book. Notify your vet if the number of placentas is less than the number of pups.
- 12-24 hours after the last birth, a vet can do a postpartum checkup to verify there are no retained pups or placentas.

Possible Problem Signs Before and During Whelp

- Dam goes past 63 days gestation (especially if due date was determined by a progesterone test)
- Dark green or black discharge appearing at the vulva before the due date (not a concern once first puppy is born)
- A hemorrhagic vaginal discharge
- Dam is in obvious distress: shaking, shivering, listless
- Dam appears weak with a rectal temperature below 97°F or above 104°F
- Dam's temperature drops but no pups appear for more than 24 hours
- Two or more hours pass after first contraction and no puppy is born
- Interval of more than 2 hours between pups (up to 4-6 can be normal)
- Dam actively straining for 30-60 minutes without birth of a puppy
- Dam is in active labor and then all signs of labor stop
- Puppy is stuck in the vulva

Keep Puppies Warm (item needed: heat source)

- Keep whelping box in a warm and draft-free environment. Place a digital thermometer in box to monitor temp.
- A heat source outside the whelping box (space heater or heat lamp) is generally safer than a heating pad. If using a heating pad never set it above "low" and never place a puppy directly on pad. Keep electrical cords out of reach.
- Temperature under heat lamp should be around 80°F the first 2-3 days, then reduced to 75°-80°F. The rest of the box can be like the general whelping room temp (see below). This way mom and pups can move away from the heat source if they are too warm.
- Use a "Ready Box" as a temporary place to keep pups warm while mom is in labor birthing another puppy, while cleaning whelping box, or to carry pups to the vet if needed.

Whelping Room (item needed: thermometer to monitor air temperature in room)

- First 2 weeks: general room temp should be at 75°-80°F; then gradually reduced to 72°-75°F by 6 weeks. Do not overheat whelping area or the mom may leave her pups in search of a cooler place.
- Do not use chemical disinfectants such as Pinesol, bleach or Lysol to clean puppy area unless rinsed extremely well! Safer option: clean with steam, or mix 1 cup vinegar, 1 cup water, and 1/2 cup rubbing alcohol to make a disinfectant.

Temperature of Pups (items needed: rectal thermometer, lubricating K-Y jelly)

- Chilling is the greatest danger to a newborn A puppy temp below 96°F is worrisome.
- Warm a chilled puppy gradually (takes 2-3 hours). Never feed a chilled puppy.
- First 24 hours: pups' temp is about 94°F, and then will gradually rise to 95°, 96°, and then 97°F
- Weeks 2-4: pups' temp is 97°-99°F. After 4 weeks: temp is 100°-101.5°F (normal adult temp: 100°-102.5°F)

Monitor and Chart Pups' Weight (charts are found in this book. Item needed: scale)

- It is important to monitor a newborn's weight. Even a slight drop in weight can be detrimental to a newborn. Record puppies' weights at birth, 12 hours later, then daily until weaned. Weigh twice daily the first week.
- Pups should show a gradual gain of 5-10% of birth weight every 24 hours, and double their weight after 8-10 days. Some newborns may gain little to none the first 24 hours. Monitor closely.

IMPORTANT
Continual crying, losing, or not gaining weight is a sign that something is wrong.
Make sure each pup is nursing well and that the dam has adequate milk.

CARING FOR THE MOTHER

Wonderful puppies begin long before a mating takes place. The care given to the future mother—conditioning, a high quality diet, excellent veterinary care, health screening, time for play and a stress free life are all factors that contribute to a successful litter. The following information is a brief overview of the care needed for the mother before, during, and after whelp. It does not replace more in depth study. There are countless scenarios, from minor to life threatening that can happen. Be prepared and learn as much as possible before breeding your bitch (see Recommended Resources, page 141). Please consult a vet (or reproduction specialist) to address any questions or concerns relating to whelping, giving medications, or any information here.

Before the Mating

- A pre-breeding evaluation performed by a vet is advisable before your bitch comes into season.

- Make sure the dam is negative for heartworms and intestinal parasites prior to breeding.

- Do not vaccinate your bitch within three months prior to breeding, during pregnancy, or lactation. Make sure however that she is current on vaccines in order to pass along immunity to her pups through the placenta and then once they are born through her first milk (colostrum).

Prior to Whelp

- DEWORMING: If a fecal test is positive, deworm the bitch in order to remove as many parasites as possible prior to whelp so that round worms are not passed to the pups through the womb and later through the milk.

- Some vets recommend deworming the bitch with small animal liquid Panacur 10% starting at day 40-45 daily until two days after whelp. Other vets have a different protocol. Consult your vet for guidance. Below is the recommendation from Dr. Jean Dodds, DVM:

  Bitches should be wormed before they are bred, unless 2-3 serial fecals are negative. We do not promote or recommend worming a pregnant bitch. Her feces can be free of parasite eggs, but she can still pass on roundworms to her puppies during fetal development, as she can harbor them in her lungs, so worming her doesn't prevent it. Puppies should be checked for roundworms in their feces by 2-3 weeks and wormed with a gentle product like pyrantel pamoate.

- DIET: Feed a high quality diet and make sure your bitch has adequate calorie intake for pregnancy. Be careful not to overfeed her, however. Excessive weight gain can make the delivery more difficult.

- The first four weeks of pregnancy: feed her usual amount of adult maintenance food. Start increasing calories in week 5 by 25% and by week 9 she should be eating 50% more of a diet formulated for growth of all life stages.

- As her abdomen gets crowded with puppies, offer her several smaller meals spaced throughout the day.

- Do not give calcium supplements during pregnancy as this could lead to eclampsia (milk fever), a life threatening condition!

- EXERCISE: Birthing pups ("labor") is hard work. A bitch in good condition will most likely have an easier time to whelp. Appropriate daily exercise (i.e. short walk at her own pace) is recommended as long as her pregnancy is progressing normally. As her due date approaches shorten her walks and stay close to home.

- GROOMING: Clip long hairs around the vulva and mammary glands a few days prior to whelp. Bath her and gently try to remove the black, waxy buildup that may be present on her nipples.

- Set up the whelping box about 10 days prior to her due date and let the mom-to-be visit it several times a day to get used to it. Keep the whelping box in a warm, draft-free, quiet area of the house.

- "Accidents" in the house may occur as her due date approaches and pressure from the growing pups pushes against her bladder. More frequent potty breaks will be needed so that she may relieve herself.

- Provide extra care as she gets bigger, especially the week prior to whelp, i.e., help going up and down the stairs.

During Whelp

- A fast-absorbing calcium supplement such as Calsorb can be given to strengthen her contractions if needed.

- If the dam needs to go out to potty after dark, make sure to keep her on leash and have a flashlight and towel in case she births a puppy.

- Monitor and record the time between each birth. Watch the mom closely. Be aware of problem signs. See page 7.

After Whelp

- Clean up the mom after whelp. A full bath is not necessary. Wash off the hind area from blood and discharge.

- Keep breast area clean. Be aware of signs of canine mastitis.

- Know the signs of eclampsia (milk fever). This can occur while she is pregnant but usually occurs during the first 3 weeks after giving birth. Eclampsia is a true medical emergency. Get to the vet immediately!

- For the first week after pups are born take the mother's temperature at least once a day. An infection may be present if her temperature is 103°F or above.

- A foul smelling dark brown discharge is worrisome and could indicate a uterine infection or retained placenta. A pink bloody discharge that persists is also worrisome. Please do not hesitate to consult your vet.

- Do not overheat whelping area. Mom may leave her pups to find a cooler place.

- Make sure your bitch has plenty of water while nursing her pups.

- Feed the nursing mother a high quality dog food formulated for "growing puppies." Her calorie requirements will increase steadily as pups grow. Feed her 2 meals a day. Depending on the size of the litter, the mom may need at least double her normal calorie intake in order to produce enough milk.

- In addition to her meals, we offer our nursing mothers plain cottage cheese or yogurt once a day, as these are excellent sources of calcium and can supply beneficial bacteria. Make sure any yogurt or cottage cheese fed is ideally plain, with no artificial sweeteners/chocolate/coffee flavors.

- Gradually reduce her meal portions after week 4 in preparation for weaning pups.

I wish people would realize that animals are totally dependent on us, helpless, like children, a trust that is put upon us.
—James Herriot

CARING FOR THE PUPS

Love to a dog, is spelled T-I-M-E. Giving of our time is probably the single most important gift we'll ever give our pups—time spent socializing, training, being involved in each developmental stage, and maintaining their physical and emotional well-being. The following information is a brief overview of the care involved. It does not replace more in depth study. There are countless scenarios, from minor to life threatening that can happen to a puppy. It is important to be prepared and learn all we can about why pups die (i.e. chilling, dehydration, fading puppy syndrome, parvovirus), how to revive a weak puppy, supplemental feeding and anything related to newborn puppy care. (See Recommended Resources on page 141.) Please consult a veterinarian to address any questions or concerns relating to the information giving here. Do not give medications to your puppies without veterinary approval.

Caring for the Pups

- Prepare a "ready box" with a clean towel and heat source to welcome each pup as they are born. This box can also be used to transport pups to the vet in case of emergency. Have a heat source ready that does not need electricity.
- Keep whelping box clean and dry. Change bedding 1-2 times a day.
- The greatest risk for a newborn is in the first 2 weeks of life. Be extra vigilant. Many breeders sleep next to newborn pups for the first week to make sure pups are warm, nursing well, and that mom doesn't accidentally sit on a puppy.
- Make sure that pups are nursing soon after birth. The first milk has colostrum providing immunity for young pups against disease.
- Watch for a steady weight gain. Record weights daily in the charts provided in this book.
- Be aware of signs of dehydration (i.e. bright pink color to tongue and mucous membranes, loss of muscle tone, weakness, skin when pinched stays up in a fold)
- Pups rely on the mother to lick their anal region so they can defecate and urinate. If she is not doing this, dip a cotton ball in warm water and gently massage their anal region. If the color of the urine on the cotton ball appears dark yellow, the pup could be dehydrated.
- Pick up pups several times a day and see how they "feel." Use this time to check for anything unusual. Refer to chart on page 16 for signs of healthy pup vs. sickly pup.
- Wash hands before touching pups and ask any visitors to do the same. The nursery should be off limits to visitors, as many diseases (i.e. distemper, parvo) can be transmitted to puppies. Extra precautionary measures such as removing shoes (or changing clothes) before entering the house is also a good idea, especially after visiting the vet, pet store, dog show, or any area where dogs frequent.
- Use a damp cloth or baby wipes to keep pups clean. Be sure to wipe the anal area and the abdomen.
- Clip toenails as needed. A small pair of fingernail clippers works well.
- Docking tails, dewclaw removal, and ear cropping are optional in some breeds. Please consult your vet for more information and timing on when a procedure needs to be done.

IMPORTANT
Chilling is the greatest danger to a newborn. Keep pups in a warm, dry, draft free environment.

Weaning Pups

- Solid foods may be gradually introduced to pups around 3 weeks of age, i.e. finely ground puppy kibble mixed with warm milk replacement formula such as Esbilac or goat's milk, and/or baby rice cereal.

- By 6 weeks pups should be eating a high quality puppy food (or all stage food). This can be moistened with warm water or milk. Shredded cheese, plain cottage cheese, yogurt or scrambled eggs can be added for variety. Puppy foods are readily available for purchase. Raw and home-cooked foods are also an option.

- Feed pups 3-4 times daily. Do not overfeed as this may cause diarrhea.

- Begin weaning pups around week 5 by removing the mom for a few hours every day. Return mom to the pups at night. Begin to decrease the mothers food portions to reduce her milk production. Her milk should be dried up within 1-2 weeks as she gradually returns to her regular portions of adult maintenance food.

- Continue to be alert for signs of mastitis in the mother during the weaning process.

Deworming (charts are found in this book to record dates given)

- Most pups are born with roundworms. Consult your vet for a deworming schedule and products to use.

- Most vets recommend starting deworming pups at 2-3 weeks because of roundworm eggs passed through the dam's milk.

- Deworming guidelines set by the American Association of Veterinary Parasitologists (AAVP) and the Centers for Disease Control and Prevention (CDC): deworm pups at 2,4,6, and 8 weeks of age, then again at 12 and 16 weeks of age. Then move to 6 months, 1 year, and then follow the adult schedule.

- An alternate method used by some breeders is to have a vet run a stool sample to test for worms and only to deworm when necessary.

Vaccination Series for Puppies (charts are found in this book)

- As breeders, we play an important role in assuring that the puppies we raise are properly vaccinated. Timing is critical. However, there is not a "one size fits all" for every puppy. Discuss with your veterinarian the vaccine protocol that best takes into account the age, health, environment and lifestyle of your pups in order to maintain appropriate immunity. A thorough discussion of the kinds and schedules is beyond the scope of this book. The following is a brief summary of the guidelines for "core vaccines."

- Core Vaccines: canine distemper (CDV), canine parvovirus 2 (CPV-2), canine adenovirus 2 (CAV), and rabies. The WSAVA defines core vaccines as vaccines which "protect animals from severe, life-threatening diseases that have global distribution."

- The WSAVA Vaccination Guidelines Group (VGG) recommends the administration of three vaccine doses to pups with the final dose of these being delivered at 14–16 weeks of age or older. If a pet animal may only be permitted a single vaccination, that vaccination should be with core vaccines at 16 weeks of age or older.

- For the full text of the World Small Animal Veterinary Association (WSAVA) Guidelines, see www.wsava.org The AAHA Canine Vaccine Guidelines are available at www.aaha.org.

IMPORTANT
Check daily for signs of healthy pup vs. sick pup. See chart on page 16.

- FIRST PUPPY SHOTS: Ideally, in non-shelter situations, immunology experts recommend the initial puppy shots (CDV, CPV, CAV) to be given at 8-9 weeks of age, followed by a second vaccination 3-4 weeks later (ideally at 11-12 weeks), followed by a third vaccination given between 14-16 weeks. Visit the WSAVA web site to stay current on vaccine protocols.

- RABIES: The first rabies vaccine should be given no earlier than 12 to 16 weeks of age (but preferably not before 16 weeks), or as local law dictates.

- MINIMAL VACCINE SCHEDULE: The following chart is reprinted with permission of the author, Dr. Jean Dodds, DVM. For further education on vaccines, titer testing, changing vaccines protocols, Q & A, and more, please visit Dr. Jean Dodds' Pet Health Resources Blog at www.hemopet.org.

Dr. Jean Dodds' Vaccination Protocol (2015)

Note: The following vaccine protocol is offered for those dogs where minimal vaccinations are advisable or desirable. The schedule is one I recommend and should not be interpreted to mean that other protocols recommended by a veterinarian would be less satisfactory. It's a matter of professional judgment and choice.

Age of Pups	Vaccine Type
9–10 weeks	Distemper + Parvovirus, MLV (e.g. Intervet Progard Puppy DPV, now renamed Nobivac DPV, when Merck and Intervet merged)
14 weeks	Same as above
16–18 weeks (optional)	Same as above (optional)
20 weeks or older, if allowable by law	Rabies 1 year vaccine
1 year later	Distemper + Parvovirus, MLV (optional = serum vaccine titer)
1 year	Rabies, killed 3-year product (use a thimerosol (mercury)-free vaccine, and give 3-4 weeks apart from distemper/parvovirus booster)

Perform vaccine antibody titers for distemper and parvovirus every three years thereafter, or more often, if desired. Vaccinate for rabies virus according to the law, except where circumstances indicate that a written waiver needs to be obtained from the primary care veterinarian. In that case, a rabies antibody titer can also be performed to accompany the waiver request. See www.rabieschallengefund.org.

🐾 Remember that rabies vaccine is best given separately, at least 2 weeks apart from other vaccines.

IMPORTANT
Remind new puppy owners to complete the entire vaccination series because maternal antibodies can last 14-16 weeks making the earlier vaccines ineffective.
Suggest that a vet do an antibody titer to assess vaccine-induced protection.

Permanent Identification

- Consider permanent identification for your pups, i.e., microchip, before they leave for their new home. Don't forget to register the microchip once it has been implanted.

Choosing New Puppy Owners

- A responsible breeder takes great care in finding loving homes for each pup. See page 141, web article "A Guide to Breeding Your Dog" for more information on how to screen prospective homes and register a puppy.

- If possible, try to meet prospective new owners in person, and/or visit their home.

- Sample questions to ask prospective puppy owners:

    1. Why have you chosen this particular breed?
    2. Who will be the primary caretaker of this dog?
    3. Have you ever raised a puppy before?
    4. Does your schedule allow enough time to feed, groom, exercise, train, play with, and meet the specific needs of this breed?
    5. How many hours do you anticipate this dog being alone during the day?
    6. Do you have children? If so, how old are they?
    7. How have you prepared your children to help care for a dog?
    8. How do you feel about training and obedience?
    9. Do you have a fenced yard?
    10. Do you have any questions or concerns I can address?

- Provide New Owners with the following: feeding instructions, health records, vaccination and deworming history, a three-generational pedigree if possible, and a copy of the adoption or sales agreement/contract along with any health guarantees. Discuss these papers with new owners.

Discussion Topics to Cover With New Puppy Owners:

- Vaccinations, deworming, heartworm prevention, flea prevention, weight control, diet, ear care, grooming, exercise, health insurance options, and breed-specific health concerns
- The importance of training and ongoing socialization. For first time dog owners, suggest a good book on the topic. If possible, ask them to read it prior to bringing their puppy home. Proper training could save a dog's life.
- Spay/neuter timing (pros and cons)
- Potty Training
- Puppy-proofing a home and any other safety issues, i.e. dangerous foods
- Pet identification i.e. microchip, name tag, collar
- The importance of having a fenced yard and/or supervision on a leash
- Opportunities for dog related sports/events, i.e. obedience, rally, agility, conformation

> Training a puppy is like raising a child.
> Every single interaction is a training opportunity.
> —Ian Dunbar, DVM, Ph.D.

PUPPY DEVELOPMENT & SOCIALIZATION

While caring for our pups' physical needs we cannot forget that their need for socialization and environmental stimulation is equally important. Both body and mind require attention in order to develop properly and create wellness. This is especially true during the first 3-4 months of a pup's life, a "critical" period when learning and socialization is maximized. It can be compared to a small window of time during brain development when pups are most impressionable. Dogs that lack adequate socialization during this time are more prone to fear, aggression, separation anxiety, or other behavioral problems later in life. Hence the importance of proper "socialization," an ongoing process in which a puppy is strategically introduced to things he may encounter as an adult, such as new people, animals, stimuli, and environments. Both nature and nurture play a role in a dog's ultimate behavioral makeup. By understanding and utilizing the developmental stages puppies go through, we can come alongside what nature has given, stimulate their interests and ability to learn, and raise the best puppies possible.

The following is a brief overview of what to expect. Keep in mind that these are general guidelines. Each puppy is unique and will find his own pace. For more in-depth study visit the American Veterinary Society of Animal Behavior website to read their position statement on puppy socialization (www.AVSABonline.org).

Neo-Natal Period (birth to 14 days)

- Puppies are are born helpless, blind, deaf, and without teeth. Only the senses of touch and taste are present. They cannot regulate their body temperature and are totally dependent on their mother and littermates for warmth. They are also unable to urinate and defecate on their own and require the mother's licking. They sleep 90% of the time and nurse when awake. Eyes begin to open between days 8-14 and hearing starts to develop.

- WHAT WE CAN DO: Make sure pups are warm, eliminating, nursing well and steadily gaining weight. Trim puppy nails as needed from day 8 on.

Transitional Period (days 14-21)

- Marked neurological development. Eyes and ears are now open but with limited function, react to sound, eliminate on their own, teeth erupting. Motor skills rapidly developing, tails wag, pups become more independent, toddle and interact with littermates. Pups are gradually becoming more aware of social and environmental stimulations.

- WHAT WE CAN DO: This is a great time to introduce toys with a variety of sounds and textures to their box. Stool samples are taken to vet and/or deworming regimen begins.

Primary Socialization Period (weeks 3-5)

- All senses are now fully functioning and pups are more aware of their surroundings. They walk, paw, chew, carry objects, bark, growl, bite littermates, "play fighting" begins. Mother leaves whelping area more frequently.

- WHAT WE CAN DO: Expose pups to everyday noises, e.g., vacuum cleaner, music, TV, in a stable environment. Also, introduce pups to various clean surfaces such as wood, carpet, or tile, for short periods. Interaction between mom and pups should continue and plays an important role in a puppy's development, as well as daily human interaction and touch. During the second half of this period play behavior increases. More physical challenges are introduced (climbing, tug toys). Solid foods may be offered around 3 weeks of age. Weaning begins.

IMPORTANT
Handle puppies daily throughout each stage, gently rubbing their bodies, tummies and feet.
Remember to wash hands before handling pups.

Secondary Socialization Period (weeks 6-16)

- **WEEKS 5-7:** Curiosity is peek as pups explore, climb, and investigate new things.

- **WHAT WE CAN DO:** Expand pup's surroundings with a rich variety of stimulations as well as frequent exposure to humans. Keep learning fun and short in duration, always being careful not to over-stimulate the pup as this may cause withdrawal or excessive fear. Short car rides, first baths, grooming, i.e. introduce a soft brush, touch teeth, gums, ears, all over body, introduce "table stacking." Feed pups 3-4 times daily. Have fresh water available. Weaning is complete by 6 -1/2 weeks but pups should still be allowed playtime with the mother.

    Note: Puppies should not transition to a new home before 8 weeks of age as this could lead to problems with dog-dog relationships and other behavioral issues.

- **WEEKS 7-9:** Brains are fully functioning. Pups are able to learn most anything, but please remember they have short attention spans. Bladder control increases and they are able to sleep through the night.

- **WHAT WE CAN DO:** Introduce individual crate training, potty training, leash training, basic commands, and short periods away from mom. Around 8 weeks, a puppy is typically a mini representation of its adult silhouette. It's a wonderful opportunity to evaluate each puppy for structure and temperament as compared to the breed standard, and record your findings (space is provided in this book). First vaccinations can be given at this time.

    Note: Pups may enter a fearful stage between 8-11 weeks, i.e. fear of loud noises, strangers. Avoid frightening or painful situations such as unnecessary surgery or travel. Negative experiences can have a long term effect.

- **WEEKS 9-12:** Motor skills continue to improve. Pups are actively learning about their world, behaviors are shaped, pups pay more attention to their humans. Appropriate behavior around others begins to develop. The transition to a new home usually happens during this time.

- **WHAT WE CAN DO:** Continue to introduce positive experiences that will shape behavior patterns, coping skills, and temperament. A health exam should be completed by a vet before puppy leaves for new home. Puppy Kindergarten can be a wonderful socialization tool. Encourage new owners to discuss with their vet the best time to enroll based on the vaccines/deworming pup has received.

- **WEEKS 13-16:** This is an age of independence and testing, teething, and incessant chewing on objects. A pup's desire to please may decrease and previously learned commands may be ignored. It is recommended to keep pup on leash for safety. Most behaviorists believe that after 16 weeks of age the window for effective socialization closes. That said, amazing things can happen when kind individuals patiently help under-socialized dogs discover their potential.

- **WHAT WE CAN DO:** Provide opportunities for dog-dog relationships, meeting a variety of people, and exposure to play/training equipment to build self confidence. Remind new owners that until completion of the puppy vaccination series there is risk of disease, i.e., parvovirus. Limit pup's exposure to well-vaccinated healthy dogs, always being careful where your puppy is walked.

AFTER 16 WEEKS: Explain to new puppy owners that a dog will move through various periods of learning and development throughout its life. Encourage them to delve into each period with enthusiasm, knowledge, and expertise. The opportunities for ongoing socialization and environmental stimulation are endless, i.e. puppy classes, obedience, conformation, agility, rally, tracking, field events, freestyle, pet therapy, and simply including him in our daily routine.

By taking the time to properly socialize our puppies, and empowering new owners with knowledge, we can rest assured that we've done our very best give our pups a bright future and plant the seeds for success. Truly, this is our greatest gift as they transition to their new homes. It is now up to the new owners to water those seeds and watch their pups bloom!

HEALTHY PUP	SICKLY PUP
Feels warm to the touch	Body and mouth feel cool to the touch
Body temp first weeks, 96°–99°F rectally	Temp below 96°F (remember to warm a chilled pup slowly)
Shiny coat	Dull coat, dim and dusky in color
Quiet, only crying when hungry	Noisy, cries often, more than 15 minutes or so
Strong sucking reflex	Unable to attach to nipple or hold on to nurse
Nursing well	Not nursing
Active, roots instinctively for his food	Lying still away from the others, not rooting to nurse
If on his back, will right himself immediately	Unable to turn himself right side up
Twitchy and jerky while asleep	Lies still
Pups lie sprawled on tummy or side with head tucked toward chest	Legs pulled toward body, head may be extended, not tucked toward chest
Birth weight gains daily (doubles after 8-10 days)	Not gaining, or else losing weight
Rectal area under tails is clean	Rectal area wet, signs of runny stool, or stool caked under the tail
Skin, when pulled at back of neck, springs back into place	Skin, when pulled at back of neck, stays creased in a little tent (pup could be dehydrated)
Urine on cotton ball appears a light straw color	Urine on cotton ball appears dark yellow (pup could be dehydrated)
Umbilical cord looks clean and dry	Umbilical area has a foul odor, redness, discharge or swelling
Eye area clean (even if closed)	Eye area has discharge or drainage. If eyes open early (i.e. day 3-4) consult vet.
Respiration clear and normal	Respiration audible, lungs sound crackly, mouth open, pup is gasping for air

63 DAY PERPETUAL WHELPING CHART

63 Day Perpetual Whelping Chart

	1	2	3	4	5	6	7	8	9	10	11	12	13	14	15	16	17	18	19	20	21	22	23	24	25	26	27	28	29	30	31
Bred: Jan	1	2	3	4	5	6	7	8	9	10	11	12	13	14	15	16	17	18	19	20	21	22	23	24	25	26	27	28	29	30	31
Due: Mar	5	6	7	8	9	10	11	12	13	14	15	16	17	18	19	20	21	22	23	24	25	26	27	28	29	30	31	Apr 1	2	3	4
Bred: Feb	1	2	3	4	5	6	7	8	9	10	11	12	13	14	15	16	17	18	19	20	21	22	23	24	25	26	27	28			
Due: Apr	5	6	7	8	9	10	11	12	13	14	15	16	17	18	19	20	21	22	23	24	25	26	27	28	29	30	May 1	2			
Bred: Mar	1	2	3	4	5	6	7	8	9	10	11	12	13	14	15	16	17	18	19	20	21	22	23	24	25	26	27	28	29	30	31
Due: May	3	4	5	6	7	8	9	10	11	12	13	14	15	16	17	18	19	20	21	22	23	24	25	26	27	28	29	30	31	Jun 1	2
Bred: Apr	1	2	3	4	5	6	7	8	9	10	11	12	13	14	15	16	17	18	19	20	21	22	23	24	25	26	27	28	29	30	
Due: Jun	3	4	5	6	7	8	9	10	11	12	13	14	15	16	17	18	19	20	21	22	23	24	25	26	27	28	29	30	Jul 1	2	
Bred: May	1	2	3	4	5	6	7	8	9	10	11	12	13	14	15	16	17	18	19	20	21	22	23	24	25	26	27	28	29	30	31
Due: Jul	3	4	5	6	7	8	9	10	11	12	13	14	15	16	17	18	19	20	21	22	23	24	25	26	27	28	29	30	31	Aug 1	2
Bred: Jun	1	2	3	4	5	6	7	8	9	10	11	12	13	14	15	16	17	18	19	20	21	22	23	24	25	26	27	28	29	30	
Due: Aug	3	4	5	6	7	8	9	10	11	12	13	14	15	16	17	18	19	20	21	22	23	24	25	26	27	28	29	30	31	Sep 1	
Bred: Jul	1	2	3	4	5	6	7	8	9	10	11	12	13	14	15	16	17	18	19	20	21	22	23	24	25	26	27	28	29	30	31
Due: Sep	2	3	4	5	6	7	8	9	10	11	12	13	14	15	16	17	18	19	20	21	22	23	24	25	26	27	28	29	30	Oct 1	2
Bred: Aug	1	2	3	4	5	6	7	8	9	10	11	12	13	14	15	16	17	18	19	20	21	22	23	24	25	26	27	28	29	30	31
Due: Oct	3	4	5	6	7	8	9	10	11	12	13	14	15	16	17	18	19	20	21	22	23	24	25	26	27	28	29	30	31	Nov 1	2
Bred: Sep	1	2	3	4	5	6	7	8	9	10	11	12	13	14	15	16	17	18	19	20	21	22	23	24	25	26	27	28	29	30	
Due: Nov	3	4	5	6	7	8	9	10	11	12	13	14	15	16	17	18	19	20	21	22	23	24	25	26	27	28	29	30	Dec 1	2	
Bred: Oct	1	2	3	4	5	6	7	8	9	10	11	12	13	14	15	16	17	18	19	20	21	22	23	24	25	26	27	28	29	30	31
Due: Dec	3	4	5	6	7	8	9	10	11	12	13	14	15	16	17	18	19	20	21	22	23	24	25	26	27	28	29	30	31	Jan 1	2
Bred: Nov	1	2	3	4	5	6	7	8	9	10	11	12	13	14	15	16	17	18	19	20	21	22	23	24	25	26	27	28	29	30	
Due: Jan	3	4	5	6	7	8	9	10	11	12	13	14	15	16	17	18	19	20	21	22	23	24	25	26	27	28	29	30	31	Feb 1	
Bred: Dec	1	2	3	4	5	6	7	8	9	10	11	12	13	14	15	16	17	18	19	20	21	22	23	24	25	26	27	28	29	30	31
Due: Feb	2	3	4	5	6	7	8	9	10	11	12	13	14	15	16	17	18	19	20	21	22	23	24	25	26	27	28	Mar 1	2	3	4

I think dogs are the most amazing creatures; they give unconditional love.
For me, they are the role model for being alive.

—Gilda Radner

PHOTO MEMORY OF A PRECIOUS LITTER

Sire _____ Dam _____ Litter DOB _____

DAM INFORMATION

Name _____ DOB _____

AKC# _____ Other registry # _____

Breed _____ Color/Markings _____

DNA# _____ Microchip# _____

Owner(s) Name _____ Telephone _____

Address _____ E-mail _____

Breeder(s)Name _____ Telephone _____

Address _____ E-mail _____

Date of Acquisition _____ Date & Duration of Lease, if any _____

Health Tests completed (i.e., OFA, CERF) _____

_____

_____

_____

_____

SIRE INFORMATION

Name _____ DOB _____

AKC# _____ Other registry # _____

Breed _____ Color/Markings _____

DNA# _____ Microchip# _____

Owner(s) Name _____ Telephone _____

Address _____ E-mail _____

Breeder(s)Name _____ Telephone _____

Address _____ E-mail _____

Date of Acquisition _____

Health Tests completed (i.e., OFA, CERF) _____

_____

_____

_____

_____

PREPARING FOR WHELP

Sire_____ Dam_____

Breeding Dates: _____ Natural/AI _____

Place of Mating _____ Persons Handling the Mating _____

Ultrasound/Radiograph results:_____ Due Date: _____

Fecal test results: _____

Monitor Dam's Temperature a week prior to whelp—see page 6

DATE:_____Temp AM _____Temp Midday _____Temp PM_____Temp Nighttime _____

DATE:_____Temp AM _____Temp Midday _____Temp PM_____Temp Nighttime _____

DATE:_____Temp AM _____Temp Midday _____Temp PM_____Temp Nighttime _____

DATE:_____Temp AM _____Temp Midday _____Temp PM_____Temp Nighttime _____

DATE:_____Temp AM _____Temp Midday _____Temp PM_____Temp Nighttime _____

DATE:_____Temp AM _____Temp Midday _____Temp PM_____Temp Nighttime _____

DATE:_____Temp AM _____Temp Midday _____Temp PM_____Temp Nighttime _____

WARNING! Some mothers-to-be may not show a temperature drop or give prior warning before giving birth. In the week preceding her due date it is strongly advised not to leave her unattended day or night.

Notes _____
_____
_____
_____
_____
_____

Watch for temperature drop to 99ºF or below, or 2 degrees below her normal temperature.

THE PUPS HAVE ARRIVED!

Sire_____ Dam_____

Hard labor begins _____ Water bag appears _____ Litter DOB _____

Refer to pages 6–7 for signs of impending whelp and stages of labor. Also Recommended Resources, page 141.

Puppy #	Time	Sex	Weight	Afterbirth?	Status	Color/Markings
1						
2						
3						
4						
5						
6						
7						
8						
9						
10						

Additional Notes

_____
_____
_____
_____
_____
_____

PUPPY WEIGHT CHART

Sire _____   Dam _____   Litter DOB _____

It is recommended to weigh your pups twice daily for the first week. See page 7.

Day / Pup#	1 am	1 pm	2 am	2 pm	3 am	3 pm	4 am	4 pm	5 am	5 pm	6 am	6 pm	7 am	7 pm	8	9
1																
2																
3																
4																
5																
6																
7																
8																
9																
10																

Notes

_____

_____

_____

_____

_____

_____

_____

PUPPY WEIGHT CHART

Sire _____ Dam _____ Litter DOB _____

See page 7.

Day / Pup#	10	11	12	13	14	15	16	17	18	19	20	21
1												
2												
3												
4												
5												
6												
7												
8												
9												
10												

Notes
_____
_____
_____
_____
_____
_____
_____

DEWORMING & VACCINES

Sire _____ Dam _____ Litter DOB _____

Vets recommend starting deworming pups at 2–3 weeks because of roundworm eggs passed through the milk.
Pups should be vaccinated to prevent diseases. Follow the schedule recommended by your vet. See pages 11–12.

| | Date Dewormed | | | | | Vaccines Vaccine #1 | Vaccine #2 | Vaccine #3 |
| | | | | | | Vaccine Name / Date | Vaccine Name / Date | Vaccine Name / Date |
Date \ Pup#	week#	week#	week#	week#	week#			
1								
2								
3								
4								
5								
6								
7								
8								
9								
10								

PUPPY EVALUATION NOTES

Sire _____ Dam _____ Litter DOB _____

Puppy evaluation is an ongoing process that begins at birth. Use this page to record your observations about structure and temperament while pups' are standing, playing, and running free. Around 8 weeks of age a puppy is typically a mini representation of their adult silhouette. It's a wonderful opportunity to evaluate each puppy in more detail. Breed-specific and general knowledge of dogs is necessary in order to correctly evaluate your litter. Refer to the official breed standard for guidance. See page 141, Recommended Resources.

_____
_____
_____
_____
_____
_____
_____
_____
_____
_____
_____
_____
_____
_____
_____
_____
_____
_____
_____
_____
_____
_____
_____

The whole is greater than the sum of its parts. —Aristotle

PUPPY/OWNER INFORMATION

Sire _____ Dam _____

Litter Date of Birth _____ # of males _____ # of females _____ Litter Reg # _____

Pup #1 Name _____ Litter # _____

Microchip _____ Color/Markings _____

Owner(s) Name _____ Tel _____

Address _____ E-mail _____

Co-owner(s) Name _____ Tel _____

Address _____ E-mail _____

Date of Sale/Gift _____ Limited/Full Registration _____ Date Deceased _____

Pup #2 Name _____ Litter # _____

Microchip _____ Color/Markings _____

Owner(s) Name _____ Tel _____

Address _____ E-mail _____

Co-owner(s) Name _____ Tel _____

Address _____ E-mail _____

Date of Sale/Gift _____ Limited/Full Registration _____ Date Deceased _____

Pup #3 Name _____ Litter # _____

Microchip _____ Color/Markings _____

Owner(s) Name _____ Tel _____

Address _____ E-mail _____

Co-owner(s) Name _____ Tel _____

Address _____ E-mail _____

Date of Sale/Gift _____ Limited/Full Registration _____ Date Deceased _____

Pup #4 Name _____ Litter # _____

Microchip _____ Color/Markings _____

Owner(s) Name _____ Tel _____

Address _____ E-mail _____

Co-owner(s) Name _____ Tel _____

Address _____ E-mail _____

Date of Sale/Gift _____ Limited/Full Registration _____ Date Deceased _____

Pup #5 Name _____ Litter # _____

Microchip _____ Color/Markings _____

Owner(s) Name _____ Tel _____

Address _____ E-mail _____

Co-owner(s) Name _____ Tel _____

Address _____ E-mail _____

Date of Sale/Gift _____ Limited/Full Registration _____ Date Deceased _____

Properly trained, a man can be a dog's best friend. —Corey Ford

Sire _____ Dam _____

Litter Date of Birth _____ # of males _____ # of females _____ Litter Reg # _____

Pup #6 Name _____ Litter # _____

Microchip _____ Color/Markings _____

Owner(s) Name _____ Tel _____

Address _____ E-mail _____

Co-owner(s) Name _____ Tel _____

Address _____ E-mail _____

Date of Sale/Gift _____ Limited/Full Registration _____ Date Deceased _____

Pup #7 Name _____ Litter # _____

Microchip _____ Color/Markings _____

Owner(s) Name _____ Tel _____

Address _____ E-mail _____

Co-owner(s) Name _____ Tel _____

Address _____ E-mail _____

Date of Sale/Gift _____ Limited/Full Registration _____ Date Deceased _____

Pup #8 Name _____ Litter # _____

Microchip _____ Color/Markings _____

Owner(s) Name _____ Tel _____

Address _____ E-mail _____

Co-owner(s) Name _____ Tel _____

Address _____ E-mail _____

Date of Sale/Gift _____ Limited/Full Registration _____ Date Deceased _____

Pup #9 Name _____ Litter # _____

Microchip _____ Color/Markings _____

Owner(s) Name _____ Tel _____

Address _____ E-mail _____

Co-owner(s) Name _____ Tel _____

Address _____ E-mail _____

Date of Sale/Gift _____ Limited/Full Registration _____ Date Deceased _____

Pup #10 Name _____ Litter # _____

Microchip _____ Color/Markings _____

Owner(s) Name _____ Tel _____

Address _____ E-mail _____

Co-owner(s) Name _____ Tel _____

Address _____ E-mail _____

Date of Sale/Gift _____ Limited/Full Registration _____ Date Deceased _____

PHOTO MEMORY OF A PRECIOUS LITTER

Sire _____ Dam _____ Litter DOB _____

DAM INFORMATION

Name _____ DOB _____

AKC# _____ Other registry # _____

Breed _____ Color/Markings _____

DNA# _____ Microchip# _____

Owner(s) Name _____ Telephone _____

Address _____ E-mail _____

Breeder(s)Name _____ Telephone _____

Address _____ E-mail _____

Date of Acquisition _____ Date & Duration of Lease, if any _____

Health Tests completed (i.e., OFA, CERF) _____

_____

_____

_____

_____

SIRE INFORMATION

Name _____ DOB _____

AKC# _____ Other registry # _____

Breed _____ Color/Markings _____

DNA# _____ Microchip# _____

Owner(s) Name _____ Telephone _____

Address _____ E-mail _____

Breeder(s)Name _____ Telephone _____

Address _____ E-mail _____

Date of Acquisition _____

Health Tests completed (i.e., OFA, CERF) _____

_____

_____

_____

_____

PREPARING FOR WHELP

Sire_____ Dam_____

Breeding Dates: _____ Natural/AI _____

Place of Mating _____ Persons Handling the Mating _____

Ultrasound/Radiograph results:_____ Due Date: _____

Fecal test results: _____

Monitor Dam's Temperature a week prior to whelp—see page 6

DATE:_____Temp AM _____Temp Midday _____Temp PM_____Temp Nighttime _____

DATE:_____Temp AM _____Temp Midday _____Temp PM_____Temp Nighttime _____

DATE:_____Temp AM _____Temp Midday _____Temp PM_____Temp Nighttime _____

DATE:_____Temp AM _____Temp Midday _____Temp PM_____Temp Nighttime _____

DATE:_____Temp AM _____Temp Midday _____Temp PM_____Temp Nighttime _____

DATE:_____Temp AM _____Temp Midday _____Temp PM_____Temp Nighttime _____

DATE:_____Temp AM _____Temp Midday _____Temp PM_____Temp Nighttime _____

WARNING! Some mothers-to-be may not show a temperature drop or give prior warning before giving birth. In the week preceding her due date it is strongly advised not to leave her unattended day or night.

Notes _____

_____

_____

_____

_____

_____

Watch for temperature drop to 99ºF or below, or 2 degrees below her normal temperature.

THE PUPS HAVE ARRIVED!

Sire_____ Dam_____

Hard labor begins _____ Water bag appears _____ Litter DOB _____

Refer to pages 6–7 for signs of impending whelp and stages of labor. Also Recommended Resources, page 141.

Puppy #	Time	Sex	Weight	Afterbirth?	Status	Color/Markings
1						
2						
3						
4						
5						
6						
7						
8						
9						
10						

Additional Notes

_____

_____

_____

_____

_____

PUPPY WEIGHT CHART

Sire _____ Dam _____ Litter DOB _____

It is recommended to weigh your pups twice daily for the first week. See page 7.

Day / Pup#	1		2		3		4		5		6		7		8	9
	am	pm	am	pm	am	pm	am	pm	am	pm	am	pm	am	pm		
1																
2	am	pm	am	pm	am	pm	am	pm	am	pm	am	pm	am	pm		
3	am	pm	am	pm	am	pm	am	pm	am	pm	am	pm	am	pm		
4	am	pm	am	pm	am	pm	am	pm	am	pm	am	pm	am	pm		
5	am	pm	am	pm	am	pm	am	pm	am	pm	am	pm	am	pm		
6	am	pm	am	pm	am	pm	am	pm	am	pm	am	pm	am	pm		
7	am	pm	am	pm	am	pm	am	pm	am	pm	am	pm	am	pm		
8	am	pm	am	pm	am	pm	am	pm	am	pm	am	pm	am	pm		
9	am	pm	am	pm	am	pm	am	pm	am	pm	am	pm	am	pm		
10	am	pm	am	pm	am	pm	am	pm	am	pm	am	pm	am	pm		

Notes

_____

_____

_____

_____

_____

_____

_____

PUPPY WEIGHT CHART

Sire _____ Dam _____ Litter DOB _____

See page 7.

Day Pup#	10	11	12	13	14	15	16	17	18	19	20	21
1												
2												
3												
4												
5												
6												
7												
8												
9												
10												

Notes

_____

_____

_____

_____

_____

_____

_____

_____

DEWORMING & VACCINES

Sire _____ Dam _____ Litter DOB _____

Vets recommend starting deworming pups at 2–3 weeks because of roundworm eggs passed through the milk.
Pups should be vaccinated to prevent diseases. Follow the schedule recommended by your vet. See pages 11–12.

Date Dewormed   ## Vaccines

Date / Pup#	week#	week#	week#	week#	week#	Vaccine #1 Vaccine Name / Date	Vaccine #2 Vaccine Name / Date	Vaccine #3 Vaccine Name / Date
1								
2								
3								
4								
5								
6								
7								
8								
9								
10								

PUPPY EVALUATION NOTES

Sire _____ Dam _____ Litter DOB _____

Puppy evaluation is an ongoing process that begins at birth. Use this page to record your observations about structure and temperament while pups' are standing, playing, and running free. Around 8 weeks of age a puppy is typically a mini representation of their adult silhouette. It's a wonderful opportunity to evaluate each puppy in more detail. Breed-specific and general knowledge of dogs is necessary in order to correctly evaluate your litter. Refer to the official breed standard for guidance. See page 141, Recommended Resources.

_____
_____
_____
_____
_____
_____
_____
_____
_____
_____
_____
_____
_____
_____
_____
_____
_____
_____
_____
_____
_____
_____

The whole is greater than the sum of its parts. —Aristotle

PUPPY/OWNER INFORMATION

Sire _____ Dam _____

Litter Date of Birth _____ # of males_____ # of females _____ Litter Reg # _____

Pup #1 Name _____ Litter # _____

Microchip _____Color/Markings _____

Owner(s) Name _____ Tel _____

Address _____ E-mail _____

Co-owner(s) Name _____ Tel _____

Address _____ E-mail _____

Date of Sale/Gift _____ Limited/Full Registration _____ Date Deceased _____

Pup #2 Name _____ Litter # _____

Microchip _____Color/Markings _____

Owner(s) Name _____ Tel _____

Address _____ E-mail _____

Co-owner(s) Name _____ Tel _____

Address _____ E-mail _____

Date of Sale/Gift _____ Limited/Full Registration _____ Date Deceased _____

Pup #3 Name _____ Litter # _____

Microchip _____Color/Markings _____

Owner(s) Name _____ Tel _____

Address _____ E-mail _____

Co-owner(s) Name _____ Tel _____

Address _____ E-mail _____

Date of Sale/Gift _____ Limited/Full Registration _____ Date Deceased _____

Pup #4 Name _____ Litter # _____

Microchip _____Color/Markings _____

Owner(s) Name _____ Tel _____

Address _____ E-mail _____

Co-owner(s) Name _____ Tel _____

Address _____ E-mail _____

Date of Sale/Gift _____ Limited/Full Registration _____ Date Deceased _____

Pup #5 Name _____ Litter # _____

Microchip _____Color/Markings _____

Owner(s) Name _____ Tel _____

Address _____ E-mail _____

Co-owner(s) Name _____ Tel _____

Address _____ E-mail _____

Date of Sale/Gift _____ Limited/Full Registration _____ Date Deceased _____

Properly trained, a man can be a dog's best friend. —Corey Ford

Sire _____ Dam _____

Litter Date of Birth _____ # of males _____ # of females _____ Litter Reg # _____

Pup #6 Name _____ Litter # _____

Microchip _____ Color/Markings _____

Owner(s) Name _____ Tel _____

Address _____ E-mail _____

Co-owner(s) Name _____ Tel _____

Address _____ E-mail _____

Date of Sale/Gift _____ Limited/Full Registration _____ Date Deceased _____

Pup #7 Name _____ Litter # _____

Microchip _____ Color/Markings _____

Owner(s) Name _____ Tel _____

Address _____ E-mail _____

Co-owner(s) Name _____ Tel _____

Address _____ E-mail _____

Date of Sale/Gift _____ Limited/Full Registration _____ Date Deceased _____

Pup #8 Name _____ Litter # _____

Microchip _____ Color/Markings _____

Owner(s) Name _____ Tel _____

Address _____ E-mail _____

Co-owner(s) Name _____ Tel _____

Address _____ E-mail _____

Date of Sale/Gift _____ Limited/Full Registration _____ Date Deceased _____

Pup #9 Name _____ Litter # _____

Microchip _____ Color/Markings _____

Owner(s) Name _____ Tel _____

Address _____ E-mail _____

Co-owner(s) Name _____ Tel _____

Address _____ E-mail _____

Date of Sale/Gift _____ Limited/Full Registration _____ Date Deceased _____

Pup #10 Name _____ Litter # _____

Microchip _____ Color/Markings _____

Owner(s) Name _____ Tel _____

Address _____ E-mail _____

Co-owner(s) Name _____ Tel _____

Address _____ E-mail _____

Date of Sale/Gift _____ Limited/Full Registration _____ Date Deceased _____

PHOTO MEMORY OF A PRECIOUS LITTER

Sire _____ Dam _____ Litter DOB _____

DAM INFORMATION

Name _____ DOB _____

AKC# _____ Other registry # _____

Breed _____ Color/Markings _____

DNA# _____ Microchip# _____

Owner(s) Name _____ Telephone _____

Address _____ E-mail _____

Breeder(s)Name _____ Telephone _____

Address _____ E-mail _____

Date of Acquisition _____ Date & Duration of Lease, if any _____

Health Tests completed (i.e., OFA, CERF) _____

_____

_____

_____

_____

SIRE INFORMATION

Name _____ DOB _____

AKC# _____ Other registry # _____

Breed _____ Color/Markings _____

DNA# _____ Microchip# _____

Owner(s) Name _____ Telephone _____

Address _____ E-mail _____

Breeder(s)Name _____ Telephone _____

Address _____ E-mail _____

Date of Acquisition _____

Health Tests completed (i.e., OFA, CERF) _____

_____

_____

_____

_____

PREPARING FOR WHELP

Sire_____ Dam_____

Breeding Dates: _____ Natural/AI _____

Place of Mating _____ Persons Handling the Mating _____

Ultrasound/Radiograph results:_____ Due Date: _____

Fecal test results: _____

Monitor Dam's Temperature a week prior to whelp—see page 6

DATE:_____Temp AM _____Temp Midday _____Temp PM_____Temp Nighttime _____

DATE:_____Temp AM _____Temp Midday _____Temp PM_____Temp Nighttime _____

DATE:_____Temp AM _____Temp Midday _____Temp PM_____Temp Nighttime _____

DATE:_____Temp AM _____Temp Midday _____Temp PM_____Temp Nighttime _____

DATE:_____Temp AM _____Temp Midday _____Temp PM_____Temp Nighttime _____

DATE:_____Temp AM _____Temp Midday _____Temp PM_____Temp Nighttime _____

DATE:_____Temp AM _____Temp Midday _____Temp PM_____Temp Nighttime _____

WARNING! Some mothers-to-be may not show a temperature drop or give prior warning before giving birth. In the week preceding her due date it is strongly advised not to leave her unattended day or night.

Notes_____

_____

_____

_____

Watch for temperature drop to 99ºF or below, or 2 degrees below her normal temperature.

_____

_____

THE PUPS HAVE ARRIVED!

Sire _____ Dam _____

Hard labor begins _____ Water bag appears _____ Litter DOB _____

Refer to pages 6–7 for signs of impending whelp and stages of labor. Also Recommended Resources, page 141.

Puppy #	Time	Sex	Weight	Afterbirth?	Status	Color/Markings
1						
2						
3						
4						
5						
6						
7						
8						
9						
10						

Additional Notes

_____

_____

_____

_____

_____

_____

PUPPY WEIGHT CHART

Sire _____ Dam _____ Litter DOB _____

It is recommended to weigh your pups twice daily for the first week. See page 7.

Day / Pup#	1		2		3		4		5		6		7		8	9
1	am	pm	am	pm	am	pm	am	pm	am	pm	am	pm	am	pm		
2	am	pm	am	pm	am	pm	am	pm	am	pm	am	pm	am	pm		
3	am	pm	am	pm	am	pm	am	pm	am	pm	am	pm	am	pm		
4	am	pm	am	pm	am	pm	am	pm	am	pm	am	pm	am	pm		
5	am	pm	am	pm	am	pm	am	pm	am	pm	am	pm	am	pm		
6	am	pm	am	pm	am	pm	am	pm	am	pm	am	pm	am	pm		
7	am	pm	am	pm	am	pm	am	pm	am	pm	am	pm	am	pm		
8	am	pm	am	pm	am	pm	am	pm	am	pm	am	pm	am	pm		
9	am	pm	am	pm	am	pm	am	pm	am	pm	am	pm	am	pm		
10	am	pm	am	pm	am	pm	am	pm	am	pm	am	pm	am	pm		

Notes

_____

_____

_____

_____

_____

_____

_____

PUPPY WEIGHT CHART

Sire _____ Dam _____ Litter DOB _____

See page 7.

Day / Pup#	10	11	12	13	14	15	16	17	18	19	20	21
1												
2												
3												
4												
5												
6												
7												
8												
9												
10												

Notes
_____
_____
_____
_____
_____
_____
_____

DEWORMING & VACCINES

Sire _____ Dam _____ Litter DOB _____

Vets recommend starting deworming pups at 2–3 weeks because of roundworm eggs passed through the milk.
Pups should be vaccinated to prevent diseases. Follow the schedule recommended by your vet. See pages 11–12.

Date Dewormed						Vaccines		
						Vaccine #1	Vaccine #2	Vaccine #3
Date / Pup#	week#	week#	week#	week#	week#	Vaccine Name / Date	Vaccine Name / Date	Vaccine Name / Date
1								
2								
3								
4								
5								
6								
7								
8								
9								
10								

PUPPY EVALUATION NOTES

Sire _____ Dam _____ Litter DOB _____

Puppy evaluation is an ongoing process that begins at birth. Use this page to record your observations about structure and temperament while pups' are standing, playing, and running free. Around 8 weeks of age a puppy is typically a mini representation of their adult silhouette. It's a wonderful opportunity to evaluate each puppy in more detail. Breed-specific and general knowledge of dogs is necessary in order to correctly evaluate your litter. Refer to the official breed standard for guidance. See page 141, Recommended Resources.

_____

_____

_____

_____

_____

_____

_____

_____

_____

_____

_____

_____

_____

_____

_____

_____

_____

_____

_____

_____

_____

_____

_____

_____

_____

The whole is greater than the sum of its parts. —Aristotle

46

PUPPY/OWNER INFORMATION

Sire _____ Dam _____

Litter Date of Birth _____ # of males _____ # of females _____ Litter Reg # _____

Pup #1 Name _____ Litter # _____

Microchip _____ Color/Markings _____

Owner(s) Name _____ Tel _____

Address _____ E-mail _____

Co-owner(s) Name _____ Tel _____

Address _____ E-mail _____

Date of Sale/Gift _____ Limited/Full Registration _____ Date Deceased _____

Pup #2 Name _____ Litter # _____

Microchip _____ Color/Markings _____

Owner(s) Name _____ Tel _____

Address _____ E-mail _____

Co-owner(s) Name _____ Tel _____

Address _____ E-mail _____

Date of Sale/Gift _____ Limited/Full Registration _____ Date Deceased _____

Pup #3 Name _____ Litter # _____

Microchip _____ Color/Markings _____

Owner(s) Name _____ Tel _____

Address _____ E-mail _____

Co-owner(s) Name _____ Tel _____

Address _____ E-mail _____

Date of Sale/Gift _____ Limited/Full Registration _____ Date Deceased _____

Pup #4 Name _____ Litter # _____

Microchip _____ Color/Markings _____

Owner(s) Name _____ Tel _____

Address _____ E-mail _____

Co-owner(s) Name _____ Tel _____

Address _____ E-mail _____

Date of Sale/Gift _____ Limited/Full Registration _____ Date Deceased _____

Pup #5 Name _____ Litter # _____

Microchip _____ Color/Markings _____

Owner(s) Name _____ Tel _____

Address _____ E-mail _____

Co-owner(s) Name _____ Tel _____

Address _____ E-mail _____

Date of Sale/Gift _____ Limited/Full Registration _____ Date Deceased _____

Properly trained, a man can be a dog's best friend. —Corey Ford

Sire _____ Dam _____

Litter Date of Birth _____ # of males _____ # of females _____ Litter Reg # _____

Pup #6 Name _____ Litter # _____

Microchip _____ Color/Markings _____

Owner(s) Name _____ Tel _____

Address _____ E-mail _____

Co-owner(s) Name _____ Tel _____

Address _____ E-mail _____

Date of Sale/Gift _____ Limited/Full Registration _____ Date Deceased _____

Pup #7 Name _____ Litter # _____

Microchip _____ Color/Markings _____

Owner(s) Name _____ Tel _____

Address _____ E-mail _____

Co-owner(s) Name _____ Tel _____

Address _____ E-mail _____

Date of Sale/Gift _____ Limited/Full Registration _____ Date Deceased _____

Pup #8 Name _____ Litter # _____

Microchip _____ Color/Markings _____

Owner(s) Name _____ Tel _____

Address _____ E-mail _____

Co-owner(s) Name _____ Tel _____

Address _____ E-mail _____

Date of Sale/Gift _____ Limited/Full Registration _____ Date Deceased _____

Pup #9 Name _____ Litter # _____

Microchip _____ Color/Markings _____

Owner(s) Name _____ Tel _____

Address _____ E-mail _____

Co-owner(s) Name _____ Tel _____

Address _____ E-mail _____

Date of Sale/Gift _____ Limited/Full Registration _____ Date Deceased _____

Pup #10 Name _____ Litter # _____

Microchip _____ Color/Markings _____

Owner(s) Name _____ Tel _____

Address _____ E-mail _____

Co-owner(s) Name _____ Tel _____

Address _____ E-mail _____

Date of Sale/Gift _____ Limited/Full Registration _____ Date Deceased _____

PHOTO MEMORY OF A PRECIOUS LITTER

Sire _____ Dam _____ Litter DOB _____

DAM INFORMATION

Name _____ DOB _____

AKC# _____ Other registry # _____

Breed _____ Color/Markings _____

DNA# _____ Microchip# _____

Owner(s) Name _____ Telephone _____

Address _____ E-mail _____

Breeder(s)Name _____ Telephone _____

Address _____ E-mail _____

Date of Acquisition _____ Date & Duration of Lease, if any _____

Health Tests completed (i.e., OFA, CERF) _____

_____

_____

_____

_____

SIRE INFORMATION

Name _____ DOB _____

AKC# _____ Other registry # _____

Breed _____ Color/Markings _____

DNA# _____ Microchip# _____

Owner(s) Name _____ Telephone _____

Address _____ E-mail _____

Breeder(s)Name _____ Telephone _____

Address _____ E-mail _____

Date of Acquisition _____

Health Tests completed (i.e., OFA, CERF) _____

_____

_____

_____

_____

PREPARING FOR WHELP

Sire_____ Dam_____

Breeding Dates: _____ Natural/AI _____

Place of Mating _____ Persons Handling the Mating _____

Ultrasound/Radiograph results:_____ Due Date: _____

Fecal test results: _____

Monitor Dam's Temperature a week prior to whelp—see page 6

DATE:_____Temp AM _____Temp Midday _____Temp PM_____Temp Nighttime _____

DATE:_____Temp AM _____Temp Midday _____Temp PM_____Temp Nighttime _____

DATE:_____Temp AM _____Temp Midday _____Temp PM_____Temp Nighttime _____

DATE:_____Temp AM _____Temp Midday _____Temp PM_____Temp Nighttime _____

DATE:_____Temp AM _____Temp Midday _____Temp PM_____Temp Nighttime _____

DATE:_____Temp AM _____Temp Midday _____Temp PM_____Temp Nighttime _____

DATE:_____Temp AM _____Temp Midday _____Temp PM_____Temp Nighttime _____

WARNING! Some mothers-to-be may not show a temperature drop or give prior warning before giving birth. In the week preceding her due date it is strongly advised not to leave her unattended day or night.

Notes _____

_____

_____

_____

_____

_____

Watch for temperature drop to 99ºF or below, or 2 degrees below her normal temperature.

THE PUPS HAVE ARRIVED!

Sire_____ Dam_____

Hard labor begins _____ Water bag appears _____ Litter DOB _____

Refer to pages 6–7 for signs of impending whelp and stages of labor. Also Recommended Resources, page 141.

Puppy #	Time	Sex	Weight	Afterbirth?	Status	Color/Markings
1						
2						
3						
4						
5						
6						
7						
8						
9						
10						

Additional Notes
_____
_____
_____
_____
_____
_____

PUPPY WEIGHT CHART

Sire _____ Dam _____ Litter DOB _____

It is recommended to weigh your pups twice daily for the first week. See page 7.

Day \ Pup#	1		2		3		4		5		6		7		8	9
	am	pm	am	pm	am	pm	am	pm	am	pm	am	pm	am	pm		
1	am	pm	am	pm	am	pm	am	pm	am	pm	am	pm	am	pm		
2	am	pm	am	pm	am	pm	am	pm	am	pm	am	pm	am	pm		
3	am	pm	am	pm	am	pm	am	pm	am	pm	am	pm	am	pm		
4	am	pm	am	pm	am	pm	am	pm	am	pm	am	pm	am	pm		
5	am	pm	am	pm	am	pm	am	pm	am	pm	am	pm	am	pm		
6	am	pm	am	pm	am	pm	am	pm	am	pm	am	pm	am	pm		
7	am	pm	am	pm	am	pm	am	pm	am	pm	am	pm	am	pm		
8	am	pm	am	pm	am	pm	am	pm	am	pm	am	pm	am	pm		
9	am	pm	am	pm	am	pm	am	pm	am	pm	am	pm	am	pm		
10	am	pm	am	pm	am	pm	am	pm	am	pm	am	pm	am	pm		

Notes

_____
_____
_____
_____
_____
_____
_____

PUPPY WEIGHT CHART

Sire _____ Dam _____ Litter DOB _____

See page 7.

Day / Pup#	10	11	12	13	14	15	16	17	18	19	20	21
1												
2												
3												
4												
5												
6												
7												
8												
9												
10												

Notes

_____

_____

_____

_____

_____

_____

_____

DEWORMING & VACCINES

Sire _____ Dam _____ Litter DOB _____

Vets recommend starting deworming pups at 2–3 weeks because of roundworm eggs passed through the milk.
Pups should be vaccinated to prevent diseases. Follow the schedule recommended by your vet. See pages 11–12.

Date Dewormed

Vaccines

Date / Pup#	week#	week#	week#	week#	week#	Vaccine #1 — Vaccine Name / Date	Vaccine #2 — Vaccine Name / Date	Vaccine #3 — Vaccine Name / Date
1								
2								
3								
4								
5								
6								
7								
8								
9								
10								

PUPPY EVALUATION NOTES

Sire _____ Dam _____ Litter DOB _____

Puppy evaluation is an ongoing process that begins at birth. Use this page to record your observations about structure and temperament while pups' are standing, playing, and running free. Around 8 weeks of age a puppy is typically a mini representation of their adult silhouette. It's a wonderful opportunity to evaluate each puppy in more detail. Breed-specific and general knowledge of dogs is necessary in order to correctly evaluate your litter. Refer to the official breed standard for guidance. See page 141, Recommended Resources.

_____
_____
_____
_____
_____
_____
_____
_____
_____
_____
_____
_____
_____
_____
_____
_____
_____
_____
_____
_____
_____
_____
_____
_____

The whole is greater than the sum of its parts. —Aristotle

PUPPY/OWNER INFORMATION

Sire _____ Dam _____

Litter Date of Birth _____ # of males _____ # of females _____ Litter Reg # _____

Pup #1 Name _____ Litter # _____

Microchip _____ Color/Markings _____

Owner(s) Name _____ Tel _____

Address _____ E-mail _____

Co-owner(s) Name _____ Tel _____

Address _____ E-mail _____

Date of Sale/Gift _____ Limited/Full Registration _____ Date Deceased _____

Pup #2 Name _____ Litter # _____

Microchip _____ Color/Markings _____

Owner(s) Name _____ Tel _____

Address _____ E-mail _____

Co-owner(s) Name _____ Tel _____

Address _____ E-mail _____

Date of Sale/Gift _____ Limited/Full Registration _____ Date Deceased _____

Pup #3 Name _____ Litter # _____

Microchip _____ Color/Markings _____

Owner(s) Name _____ Tel _____

Address _____ E-mail _____

Co-owner(s) Name _____ Tel _____

Address _____ E-mail _____

Date of Sale/Gift _____ Limited/Full Registration _____ Date Deceased _____

Pup #4 Name _____ Litter # _____

Microchip _____ Color/Markings _____

Owner(s) Name _____ Tel _____

Address _____ E-mail _____

Co-owner(s) Name _____ Tel _____

Address _____ E-mail _____

Date of Sale/Gift _____ Limited/Full Registration _____ Date Deceased _____

Pup #5 Name _____ Litter # _____

Microchip _____ Color/Markings _____

Owner(s) Name _____ Tel _____

Address _____ E-mail _____

Co-owner(s) Name _____ Tel _____

Address _____ E-mail _____

Date of Sale/Gift _____ Limited/Full Registration _____ Date Deceased _____

Properly trained, a man can be a dog's best friend. —Corey Ford

Sire _____ Dam _____

Litter Date of Birth _____ # of males _____ # of females _____ Litter Reg # _____

Pup #6 Name _____ Litter # _____

Microchip _____ Color/Markings _____

Owner(s) Name _____ Tel _____

Address _____ E-mail _____

Co-owner(s) Name _____ Tel _____

Address _____ E-mail _____

Date of Sale/Gift _____ Limited/Full Registration _____ Date Deceased _____

Pup #7 Name _____ Litter # _____

Microchip _____ Color/Markings _____

Owner(s) Name _____ Tel _____

Address _____ E-mail _____

Co-owner(s) Name _____ Tel _____

Address _____ E-mail _____

Date of Sale/Gift _____ Limited/Full Registration _____ Date Deceased _____

Pup #8 Name _____ Litter # _____

Microchip _____ Color/Markings _____

Owner(s) Name _____ Tel _____

Address _____ E-mail _____

Co-owner(s) Name _____ Tel _____

Address _____ E-mail _____

Date of Sale/Gift _____ Limited/Full Registration _____ Date Deceased _____

Pup #9 Name _____ Litter # _____

Microchip _____ Color/Markings _____

Owner(s) Name _____ Tel _____

Address _____ E-mail _____

Co-owner(s) Name _____ Tel _____

Address _____ E-mail _____

Date of Sale/Gift _____ Limited/Full Registration _____ Date Deceased _____

Pup #10 Name _____ Litter # _____

Microchip _____ Color/Markings _____

Owner(s) Name _____ Tel _____

Address _____ E-mail _____

Co-owner(s) Name _____ Tel _____

Address _____ E-mail _____

Date of Sale/Gift _____ Limited/Full Registration _____ Date Deceased _____

58

PHOTO MEMORY OF A PRECIOUS LITTER

Sire _____ Dam _____ Litter DOB _____

DAM INFORMATION

Name _____ DOB _____

AKC# _____ Other registry # _____

Breed _____ Color/Markings _____

DNA# _____ Microchip# _____

Owner(s) Name _____ Telephone _____

Address _____ E-mail _____

Breeder(s)Name _____ Telephone _____

Address _____ E-mail _____

Date of Acquisition _____ Date & Duration of Lease, if any _____

Health Tests completed (i.e., OFA, CERF) _____

_____

_____

_____

_____

SIRE INFORMATION

Name _____ DOB _____

AKC# _____ Other registry # _____

Breed _____ Color/Markings _____

DNA# _____ Microchip# _____

Owner(s) Name _____ Telephone _____

Address _____ E-mail _____

Breeder(s)Name _____ Telephone _____

Address _____ E-mail _____

Date of Acquisition _____

Health Tests completed (i.e., OFA, CERF) _____

_____

_____

_____

_____

PREPARING FOR WHELP

Sire_____ Dam_____

Breeding Dates: _____ Natural/AI _____

Place of Mating _____ Persons Handling the Mating _____

Ultrasound/Radiograph results:_____ Due Date: _____

Fecal test results: _____

Monitor Dam's Temperature a week prior to whelp—see page 6

DATE:_____Temp AM _____Temp Midday _____Temp PM_____Temp Nighttime _____

DATE:_____Temp AM _____Temp Midday _____Temp PM_____Temp Nighttime _____

DATE:_____Temp AM _____Temp Midday _____Temp PM_____Temp Nighttime _____

DATE:_____Temp AM _____Temp Midday _____Temp PM_____Temp Nighttime _____

DATE:_____Temp AM _____Temp Midday _____Temp PM_____Temp Nighttime _____

DATE:_____Temp AM _____Temp Midday _____Temp PM_____Temp Nighttime _____

DATE:_____Temp AM _____Temp Midday _____Temp PM_____Temp Nighttime _____

WARNING! Some mothers-to-be may not show a temperature drop or give prior warning before giving birth. In the week preceding her due date it is strongly advised not to leave her unattended day or night.

Notes _____

_____

_____

_____

_____

_____

Watch for temperature drop to 99ºF or below, or 2 degrees below her normal temperature.

THE PUPS HAVE ARRIVED!

Sire_____ Dam_____

Hard labor begins _____ Water bag appears _____ Litter DOB _____

Refer to pages 6–7 for signs of impending whelp and stages of labor. Also Recommended Resources, page 141.

Puppy #	Time	Sex	Weight	Afterbirth?	Status	Color/Markings
1						
2						
3						
4						
5						
6						
7						
8						
9						
10						

Additional Notes

_____

_____

_____

_____

_____

_____

PUPPY WEIGHT CHART

Sire _____   Dam _____   Litter DOB _____

It is recommended to weigh your pups twice daily for the first week. See page 7.

Day / Pup#	1 am	1 pm	2 am	2 pm	3 am	3 pm	4 am	4 pm	5 am	5 pm	6 am	6 pm	7 am	7 pm	8	9
1																
2																
3																
4																
5																
6																
7																
8																
9																
10																

Notes

_____

_____

_____

_____

_____

_____

_____

PUPPY WEIGHT CHART

Sire _____ Dam _____ Litter DOB _____

See page 7.

Day / Pup#	10	11	12	13	14	15	16	17	18	19	20	21
1												
2												
3												
4												
5												
6												
7												
8												
9												
10												

Notes
_____
_____
_____
_____
_____
_____
_____

DEWORMING & VACCINES

Sire _____ Dam _____ Litter DOB _____

Vets recommend starting deworming pups at 2–3 weeks because of roundworm eggs passed through the milk.
Pups should be vaccinated to prevent diseases. Follow the schedule recommended by your vet. See pages 11–12.

Date Dewormed   Vaccines

Date / Pup#	week#	week#	week#	week#	week#	Vaccine #1 — Vaccine Name / Date	Vaccine #2 — Vaccine Name / Date	Vaccine #3 — Vaccine Name / Date
1								
2								
3								
4								
5								
6								
7								
8								
9								
10								

PUPPY EVALUATION NOTES

Sire _____ Dam _____ Litter DOB _____

Puppy evaluation is an ongoing process that begins at birth. Use this page to record your observations about structure and temperament while pups' are standing, playing, and running free. Around 8 weeks of age a puppy is typically a mini representation of their adult silhouette. It's a wonderful opportunity to evaluate each puppy in more detail. Breed-specific and general knowledge of dogs is necessary in order to correctly evaluate your litter. Refer to the official breed standard for guidance. See page 141, Recommended Resources.

_____
_____
_____
_____
_____
_____
_____
_____
_____
_____
_____
_____
_____
_____
_____
_____
_____
_____
_____
_____
_____
_____

The whole is greater than the sum of its parts. —Aristotle

PUPPY/OWNER INFORMATION

Sire _____ Dam _____

Litter Date of Birth _____ # of males _____ # of females _____ Litter Reg # _____

Pup #1 Name _____ Litter # _____

Microchip _____ Color/Markings _____

Owner(s) Name _____ Tel _____

Address _____ E-mail _____

Co-owner(s) Name _____ Tel _____

Address _____ E-mail _____

Date of Sale/Gift _____ Limited/Full Registration _____ Date Deceased _____

Pup #2 Name _____ Litter # _____

Microchip _____ Color/Markings _____

Owner(s) Name _____ Tel _____

Address _____ E-mail _____

Co-owner(s) Name _____ Tel _____

Address _____ E-mail _____

Date of Sale/Gift _____ Limited/Full Registration _____ Date Deceased _____

Pup #3 Name _____ Litter # _____

Microchip _____ Color/Markings _____

Owner(s) Name _____ Tel _____

Address _____ E-mail _____

Co-owner(s) Name _____ Tel _____

Address _____ E-mail _____

Date of Sale/Gift _____ Limited/Full Registration _____ Date Deceased _____

Pup #4 Name _____ Litter # _____

Microchip _____ Color/Markings _____

Owner(s) Name _____ Tel _____

Address _____ E-mail _____

Co-owner(s) Name _____ Tel _____

Address _____ E-mail _____

Date of Sale/Gift _____ Limited/Full Registration _____ Date Deceased _____

Pup #5 Name _____ Litter # _____

Microchip _____ Color/Markings _____

Owner(s) Name _____ Tel _____

Address _____ E-mail _____

Co-owner(s) Name _____ Tel _____

Address _____ E-mail _____

Date of Sale/Gift _____ Limited/Full Registration _____ Date Deceased _____

Properly trained, a man can be a dog's best friend. —Corey Ford

Sire _____ Dam _____

Litter Date of Birth _____ # of males _____ # of females _____ Litter Reg # _____

Pup #6 Name _____ Litter # _____

Microchip _____ Color/Markings _____

Owner(s) Name _____ Tel _____

Address _____ E-mail _____

Co-owner(s) Name _____ Tel _____

Address_____ E-mail _____

Date of Sale/Gift _____ Limited/Full Registration _____ Date Deceased _____

Pup #7 Name _____ Litter # _____

Microchip _____ Color/Markings _____

Owner(s) Name _____ Tel _____

Address _____ E-mail _____

Co-owner(s) Name _____ Tel _____

Address_____ E-mail _____

Date of Sale/Gift _____ Limited/Full Registration _____ Date Deceased _____

Pup #8 Name _____ Litter # _____

Microchip _____ Color/Markings _____

Owner(s) Name _____ Tel _____

Address _____ E-mail _____

Co-owner(s) Name _____ Tel _____

Address_____ E-mail _____

Date of Sale/Gift _____ Limited/Full Registration _____ Date Deceased _____

Pup #9 Name _____ Litter # _____

Microchip _____ Color/Markings _____

Owner(s) Name _____ Tel _____

Address _____ E-mail _____

Co-owner(s) Name _____ Tel _____

Address_____ E-mail _____

Date of Sale/Gift _____ Limited/Full Registration _____ Date Deceased _____

Pup #10 Name _____ Litter # _____

Microchip _____ Color/Markings _____

Owner(s) Name _____ Tel _____

Address _____ E-mail _____

Co-owner(s) Name _____ Tel _____

Address_____ E-mail _____

Date of Sale/Gift _____ Limited/Full Registration _____ Date Deceased _____

PHOTO MEMORY OF A PRECIOUS LITTER

Sire _____ Dam _____ Litter DOB _____

DAM INFORMATION

Name _____ DOB _____

AKC# _____ Other registry # _____

Breed _____ Color/Markings _____

DNA# _____ Microchip# _____

Owner(s) Name _____ Telephone _____

Address _____ E-mail _____

Breeder(s)Name _____ Telephone _____

Address _____ E-mail _____

Date of Acquisition _____ Date & Duration of Lease, if any _____

Health Tests completed (i.e., OFA, CERF) _____

_____

_____

_____

_____

SIRE INFORMATION

Name _____ DOB _____

AKC# _____ Other registry # _____

Breed _____ Color/Markings _____

DNA# _____ Microchip# _____

Owner(s) Name _____ Telephone _____

Address _____ E-mail _____

Breeder(s)Name _____ Telephone _____

Address _____ E-mail _____

Date of Acquisition _____

Health Tests completed (i.e., OFA, CERF) _____

_____

_____

_____

_____

PREPARING FOR WHELP

Sire_____ Dam_____

Breeding Dates: _____ Natural/AI _____

Place of Mating _____ Persons Handling the Mating _____

Ultrasound/Radiograph results:_____ Due Date: _____

Fecal test results: _____

Monitor Dam's Temperature a week prior to whelp—see page 6

DATE:_____Temp AM _____Temp Midday _____Temp PM_____Temp Nighttime _____

DATE:_____Temp AM _____Temp Midday _____Temp PM_____Temp Nighttime _____

DATE:_____Temp AM _____Temp Midday _____Temp PM_____Temp Nighttime _____

DATE:_____Temp AM _____Temp Midday _____Temp PM_____Temp Nighttime _____

DATE:_____Temp AM _____Temp Midday _____Temp PM_____Temp Nighttime _____

DATE:_____Temp AM _____Temp Midday _____Temp PM_____Temp Nighttime _____

DATE:_____Temp AM _____Temp Midday _____Temp PM_____Temp Nighttime _____

WARNING! Some mothers-to-be may not show a temperature drop or give prior warning before giving birth. In the week preceding her due date it is strongly advised not to leave her unattended day or night.

Notes _____

_____

_____

_____

_____

_____

_____

> Watch for temperature drop to 99ºF or below, or 2 degrees below her normal temperature.

THE PUPS HAVE ARRIVED!

Sire_____ Dam_____

Hard labor begins _____ Water bag appears _____ Litter DOB _____

Refer to pages 6–7 for signs of impending whelp and stages of labor. Also Recommended Resources, page 141.

Puppy #	Time	Sex	Weight	Afterbirth?	Status	Color/Markings
1						
2						
3						
4						
5						
6						
7						
8						
9						
10						

Additional Notes
_____
_____
_____
_____
_____

PUPPY WEIGHT CHART

Sire _____ Dam _____ Litter DOB _____

It is recommended to weigh your pups twice daily for the first week. See page 7.

Day / Pup#	1		2		3		4		5		6		7		8	9
	am	pm	am	pm	am	pm	am	pm	am	pm	am	pm	am	pm		
1																
2	am	pm	am	pm	am	pm	am	pm	am	pm	am	pm	am	pm		
3	am	pm	am	pm	am	pm	am	pm	am	pm	am	pm	am	pm		
4	am	pm	am	pm	am	pm	am	pm	am	pm	am	pm	am	pm		
5	am	pm	am	pm	am	pm	am	pm	am	pm	am	pm	am	pm		
6	am	pm	am	pm	am	pm	am	pm	am	pm	am	pm	am	pm		
7	am	pm	am	pm	am	pm	am	pm	am	pm	am	pm	am	pm		
8	am	pm	am	pm	am	pm	am	pm	am	pm	am	pm	am	pm		
9	am	pm	am	pm	am	pm	am	pm	am	pm	am	pm	am	pm		
10	am	pm	am	pm	am	pm	am	pm	am	pm	am	pm	am	pm		

Notes

_____

_____

_____

_____

_____

_____

_____

PUPPY WEIGHT CHART

Sire _____ Dam _____ Litter DOB _____

See page 7.

Day / Pup#	10	11	12	13	14	15	16	17	18	19	20	21
1												
2												
3												
4												
5												
6												
7												
8												
9												
10												

Notes
_____
_____
_____
_____
_____
_____
_____

DEWORMING & VACCINES

Sire _____ Dam _____ Litter DOB _____

Vets recommend starting deworming pups at 2–3 weeks because of roundworm eggs passed through the milk.
Pups should be vaccinated to prevent diseases. Follow the schedule recommended by your vet. See pages 11–12.

Date Dewormed						Vaccines		
						Vaccine #1	Vaccine #2	Vaccine #3
Date / Pup#	week#	week#	week#	week#	week#	Vaccine Name / Date	Vaccine Name / Date	Vaccine Name / Date
1								
2								
3								
4								
5								
6								
7								
8								
9								
10								

PUPPY EVALUATION NOTES

Sire _____ Dam _____ Litter DOB _____

Puppy evaluation is an ongoing process that begins at birth. Use this page to record your observations about structure and temperament while pups' are standing, playing, and running free. Around 8 weeks of age a puppy is typically a mini representation of their adult silhouette. It's a wonderful opportunity to evaluate each puppy in more detail. Breed-specific and general knowledge of dogs is necessary in order to correctly evaluate your litter. Refer to the official breed standard for guidance. See page 141, Recommended Resources.

_____

_____

_____

_____

_____

_____

_____

_____

_____

_____

_____

_____

_____

_____

_____

_____

_____

_____

_____

_____

_____

_____

_____

The whole is greater than the sum of its parts. —Aristotle

PUPPY/OWNER INFORMATION

Sire _____ Dam _____

Litter Date of Birth _____ # of males _____ # of females _____ Litter Reg # _____

Pup #1 Name _____ Litter # _____

Microchip _____ Color/Markings _____

Owner(s) Name _____ Tel _____

Address _____ E-mail _____

Co-owner(s) Name _____ Tel _____

Address _____ E-mail _____

Date of Sale/Gift _____ Limited/Full Registration _____ Date Deceased _____

Pup #2 Name _____ Litter # _____

Microchip _____ Color/Markings _____

Owner(s) Name _____ Tel _____

Address _____ E-mail _____

Co-owner(s) Name _____ Tel _____

Address _____ E-mail _____

Date of Sale/Gift _____ Limited/Full Registration _____ Date Deceased _____

Pup #3 Name _____ Litter # _____

Microchip _____ Color/Markings _____

Owner(s) Name _____ Tel _____

Address _____ E-mail _____

Co-owner(s) Name _____ Tel _____

Address _____ E-mail _____

Date of Sale/Gift _____ Limited/Full Registration _____ Date Deceased _____

Pup #4 Name _____ Litter # _____

Microchip _____ Color/Markings _____

Owner(s) Name _____ Tel _____

Address _____ E-mail _____

Co-owner(s) Name _____ Tel _____

Address _____ E-mail _____

Date of Sale/Gift _____ Limited/Full Registration _____ Date Deceased _____

Pup #5 Name _____ Litter # _____

Microchip _____ Color/Markings _____

Owner(s) Name _____ Tel _____

Address _____ E-mail _____

Co-owner(s) Name _____ Tel _____

Address _____ E-mail _____

Date of Sale/Gift _____ Limited/Full Registration _____ Date Deceased _____

Properly trained, a man can be a dog's best friend. —Corey Ford

Sire _____ Dam _____

Litter Date of Birth _____ # of males _____ # of females _____ Litter Reg # _____

Pup #6 Name _____ Litter # _____

Microchip _____ Color/Markings _____

Owner(s) Name _____ Tel _____

Address _____ E-mail _____

Co-owner(s) Name _____ Tel _____

Address _____ E-mail _____

Date of Sale/Gift _____ Limited/Full Registration _____ Date Deceased _____

Pup #7 Name _____ Litter # _____

Microchip _____ Color/Markings _____

Owner(s) Name _____ Tel _____

Address _____ E-mail _____

Co-owner(s) Name _____ Tel _____

Address _____ E-mail _____

Date of Sale/Gift _____ Limited/Full Registration _____ Date Deceased _____

Pup #8 Name _____ Litter # _____

Microchip _____ Color/Markings _____

Owner(s) Name _____ Tel _____

Address _____ E-mail _____

Co-owner(s) Name _____ Tel _____

Address _____ E-mail _____

Date of Sale/Gift _____ Limited/Full Registration _____ Date Deceased _____

Pup #9 Name _____ Litter # _____

Microchip _____ Color/Markings _____

Owner(s) Name _____ Tel _____

Address _____ E-mail _____

Co-owner(s) Name _____ Tel _____

Address _____ E-mail _____

Date of Sale/Gift _____ Limited/Full Registration _____ Date Deceased _____

Pup #10 Name _____ Litter # _____

Microchip _____ Color/Markings _____

Owner(s) Name _____ Tel _____

Address _____ E-mail _____

Co-owner(s) Name _____ Tel _____

Address _____ E-mail _____

Date of Sale/Gift _____ Limited/Full Registration _____ Date Deceased _____

PHOTO MEMORY OF A PRECIOUS LITTER

Sire _____ Dam _____ Litter DOB _____

DAM INFORMATION

Name _____ DOB _____

AKC# _____ Other registry # _____

Breed _____ Color/Markings _____

DNA# _____ Microchip# _____

Owner(s) Name _____ Telephone _____

Address _____ E-mail _____

Breeder(s)Name _____ Telephone _____

Address _____ E-mail _____

Date of Acquisition _____ Date & Duration of Lease, if any _____

Health Tests completed (i.e., OFA, CERF) _____

_____

_____

_____

_____

_____

SIRE INFORMATION

Name _____ DOB _____

AKC# _____ Other registry # _____

Breed _____ Color/Markings _____

DNA# _____ Microchip# _____

Owner(s) Name _____ Telephone _____

Address _____ E-mail _____

Breeder(s)Name _____ Telephone _____

Address _____ E-mail _____

Date of Acquisition _____

Health Tests completed (i.e., OFA, CERF) _____

_____

_____

_____

_____

PREPARING FOR WHELP

Sire_____ Dam_____

Breeding Dates: _____ Natural/AI _____

Place of Mating _____ Persons Handling the Mating _____

Ultrasound/Radiograph results:_____ Due Date: _____

Fecal test results: _____

Monitor Dam's Temperature a week prior to whelp—see page 6

DATE:_____Temp AM _____Temp Midday _____Temp PM_____Temp Nighttime _____

DATE:_____Temp AM _____Temp Midday _____Temp PM_____Temp Nighttime _____

DATE:_____Temp AM _____Temp Midday _____Temp PM_____Temp Nighttime _____

DATE:_____Temp AM _____Temp Midday _____Temp PM_____Temp Nighttime _____

DATE:_____Temp AM _____Temp Midday _____Temp PM_____Temp Nighttime _____

DATE:_____Temp AM _____Temp Midday _____Temp PM_____Temp Nighttime _____

DATE:_____Temp AM _____Temp Midday _____Temp PM_____Temp Nighttime _____

WARNING! Some mothers-to-be may not show a temperature drop or give prior warning before giving birth. In the week preceding her due date it is strongly advised not to leave her unattended day or night.

Notes _____

_____

_____

_____

_____

_____

_____

Watch for temperature drop to 99°F or below, or 2 degrees below her normal temperature.

THE PUPS HAVE ARRIVED!

Sire_____ Dam_____

Hard labor begins _____ Water bag appears _____ Litter DOB _____

Refer to pages 6–7 for signs of impending whelp and stages of labor. Also Recommended Resources, page 141.

Puppy #	Time	Sex	Weight	Afterbirth?	Status	Color/Markings
1						
2						
3						
4						
5						
6						
7						
8						
9						
10						

Additional Notes

_____

_____

_____

_____

_____

_____

PUPPY WEIGHT CHART

Sire _____ Dam _____ Litter DOB _____

It is recommended to weigh your pups twice daily for the first week. See page 7.

Day / Pup#	1		2		3		4		5		6		7		8	9
	am	pm	am	pm	am	pm	am	pm	am	pm	am	pm	am	pm		
1																
2	am	pm	am	pm	am	pm	am	pm	am	pm	am	pm	am	pm		
3	am	pm	am	pm	am	pm	am	pm	am	pm	am	pm	am	pm		
4	am	pm	am	pm	am	pm	am	pm	am	pm	am	pm	am	pm		
5	am	pm	am	pm	am	pm	am	pm	am	pm	am	pm	am	pm		
6	am	pm	am	pm	am	pm	am	pm	am	pm	am	pm	am	pm		
7	am	pm	am	pm	am	pm	am	pm	am	pm	am	pm	am	pm		
8	am	pm	am	pm	am	pm	am	pm	am	pm	am	pm	am	pm		
9	am	pm	am	pm	am	pm	am	pm	am	pm	am	pm	am	pm		
10	am	pm	am	pm	am	pm	am	pm	am	pm	am	pm	am	pm		

Notes
_____
_____
_____
_____
_____
_____
_____

PUPPY WEIGHT CHART

Sire _____ Dam _____ Litter DOB _____

See page 7.

Day / Pup#	10	11	12	13	14	15	16	17	18	19	20	21
1												
2												
3												
4												
5												
6												
7												
8												
9												
10												

Notes
_____
_____
_____
_____
_____
_____
_____

DEWORMING & VACCINES

Sire _____ Dam _____ Litter DOB _____

Vets recommend starting deworming pups at 2–3 weeks because of roundworm eggs passed through the milk.
Pups should be vaccinated to prevent diseases. Follow the schedule recommended by your vet. See pages 11–12.

Date Dewormed						Vaccines		
						Vaccine #1	**Vaccine #2**	**Vaccine #3**
Date / Pup#	week#	week#	week#	week#	week#	Vaccine Name / Date	Vaccine Name / Date	Vaccine Name / Date
1								
2								
3								
4								
5								
6								
7								
8								
9								
10								

PUPPY EVALUATION NOTES

Sire _____ Dam _____ Litter DOB _____

Puppy evaluation is an ongoing process that begins at birth. Use this page to record your observations about structure and temperament while pups' are standing, playing, and running free. Around 8 weeks of age a puppy is typically a mini representation of their adult silhouette. It's a wonderful opportunity to evaluate each puppy in more detail. Breed-specific and general knowledge of dogs is necessary in order to correctly evaluate your litter. Refer to the official breed standard for guidance. See page 141, Recommended Resources.

_____

_____

_____

_____

_____

_____

_____

_____

_____

_____

_____

_____

_____

_____

_____

_____

_____

_____

_____

_____

_____

_____

_____

_____

_____

_____

The whole is greater than the sum of its parts. —Aristotle

PUPPY/OWNER INFORMATION

Sire _____ Dam _____

Litter Date of Birth _____ # of males _____ # of females _____ Litter Reg # _____

Pup #1 Name _____ Litter # _____

Microchip _____Color/Markings _____

Owner(s) Name _____ Tel _____

Address _____ E-mail _____

Co-owner(s) Name _____ Tel _____

Address_____ E-mail_____

Date of Sale/Gift _____ Limited/Full Registration _____ Date Deceased _____

Pup #2 Name _____ Litter # _____

Microchip _____Color/Markings _____

Owner(s) Name _____ Tel _____

Address _____ E-mail _____

Co-owner(s) Name _____ Tel _____

Address_____ E-mail_____

Date of Sale/Gift _____ Limited/Full Registration _____ Date Deceased _____

Pup #3 Name _____ Litter # _____

Microchip _____Color/Markings _____

Owner(s) Name _____ Tel _____

Address _____ E-mail _____

Co-owner(s) Name _____ Tel _____

Address_____ E-mail_____

Date of Sale/Gift _____ Limited/Full Registration _____ Date Deceased _____

Pup #4 Name _____ Litter # _____

Microchip _____Color/Markings _____

Owner(s) Name _____ Tel _____

Address _____ E-mail _____

Co-owner(s) Name _____ Tel _____

Address_____ E-mail_____

Date of Sale/Gift _____ Limited/Full Registration _____ Date Deceased _____

Pup #5 Name _____ Litter # _____

Microchip _____Color/Markings _____

Owner(s) Name _____ Tel _____

Address _____ E-mail _____

Co-owner(s) Name _____ Tel _____

Address_____ E-mail_____

Date of Sale/Gift _____ Limited/Full Registration _____ Date Deceased _____

Properly trained, a man can be a dog's best friend. —Corey Ford

Sire _____ Dam _____

Litter Date of Birth _____ # of males _____ # of females _____ Litter Reg # _____

Pup #6 Name _____ Litter # _____

Microchip _____ Color/Markings _____

Owner(s) Name _____ Tel _____

Address _____ E-mail _____

Co-owner(s) Name _____ Tel _____

Address _____ E-mail _____

Date of Sale/Gift _____ Limited/Full Registration _____ Date Deceased _____

Pup #7 Name _____ Litter # _____

Microchip _____ Color/Markings _____

Owner(s) Name _____ Tel _____

Address _____ E-mail _____

Co-owner(s) Name _____ Tel _____

Address _____ E-mail _____

Date of Sale/Gift _____ Limited/Full Registration _____ Date Deceased _____

Pup #8 Name _____ Litter # _____

Microchip _____ Color/Markings _____

Owner(s) Name _____ Tel _____

Address _____ E-mail _____

Co-owner(s) Name _____ Tel _____

Address _____ E-mail _____

Date of Sale/Gift _____ Limited/Full Registration _____ Date Deceased _____

Pup #9 Name _____ Litter # _____

Microchip _____ Color/Markings _____

Owner(s) Name _____ Tel _____

Address _____ E-mail _____

Co-owner(s) Name _____ Tel _____

Address _____ E-mail _____

Date of Sale/Gift _____ Limited/Full Registration _____ Date Deceased _____

Pup #10 Name _____ Litter # _____

Microchip _____ Color/Markings _____

Owner(s) Name _____ Tel _____

Address _____ E-mail _____

Co-owner(s) Name _____ Tel _____

Address _____ E-mail _____

Date of Sale/Gift _____ Limited/Full Registration _____ Date Deceased _____

PHOTO MEMORY OF A PRECIOUS LITTER

Sire _____ Dam _____ Litter DOB _____

DAM INFORMATION

Name _____ DOB _____

AKC# _____ Other registry # _____

Breed _____ Color/Markings _____

DNA# _____ Microchip# _____

Owner(s) Name _____ Telephone _____

Address _____ E-mail _____

Breeder(s)Name _____ Telephone _____

Address _____ E-mail _____

Date of Acquisition _____ Date & Duration of Lease, if any _____

Health Tests completed (i.e., OFA, CERF) _____

_____

_____

_____

_____

SIRE INFORMATION

Name _____ DOB _____

AKC# _____ Other registry # _____

Breed _____ Color/Markings _____

DNA# _____ Microchip# _____

Owner(s) Name _____ Telephone _____

Address _____ E-mail _____

Breeder(s)Name _____ Telephone _____

Address _____ E-mail _____

Date of Acquisition _____

Health Tests completed (i.e., OFA, CERF) _____

_____

_____

_____

_____

PREPARING FOR WHELP

Sire_____ Dam_____

Breeding Dates: _____ Natural/AI _____

Place of Mating _____ Persons Handling the Mating _____

Ultrasound/Radiograph results:_____ Due Date: _____

Fecal test results: _____

Monitor Dam's Temperature a week prior to whelp—see page 6

DATE:_____Temp AM _____Temp Midday _____Temp PM_____Temp Nighttime _____

DATE:_____Temp AM _____Temp Midday _____Temp PM_____Temp Nighttime _____

DATE:_____Temp AM _____Temp Midday _____Temp PM_____Temp Nighttime _____

DATE:_____Temp AM _____Temp Midday _____Temp PM_____Temp Nighttime _____

DATE:_____Temp AM _____Temp Midday _____Temp PM_____Temp Nighttime _____

DATE:_____Temp AM _____Temp Midday _____Temp PM_____Temp Nighttime _____

DATE:_____Temp AM _____Temp Midday _____Temp PM_____Temp Nighttime _____

WARNING! Some mothers-to-be may not show a temperature drop or give prior warning before giving birth. In the week preceding her due date it is strongly advised not to leave her unattended day or night.

Notes _____

_____

_____

_____

_____

_____

Watch for temperature drop to 99ºF or below, or 2 degrees below her normal temperature.

THE PUPS HAVE ARRIVED!

Sire_____ Dam_____

Hard labor begins _____ Water bag appears _____ Litter DOB _____

Refer to pages 6–7 for signs of impending whelp and stages of labor. Also Recommended Resources, page 141.

Puppy #	Time	Sex	Weight	Afterbirth?	Status	Color/Markings
1						
2						
3						
4						
5						
6						
7						
8						
9						
10						

Additional Notes
_____
_____
_____
_____
_____
_____

PUPPY WEIGHT CHART

Sire _____   Dam _____   Litter DOB _____

It is recommended to weigh your pups twice daily for the first week. See page 7.

Day / Pup#	1		2		3		4		5		6		7		8	9
	am	pm	am	pm	am	pm	am	pm	am	pm	am	pm	am	pm		
1																
2																
3																
4																
5																
6																
7																
8																
9																
10																

Notes

_____

_____

_____

_____

_____

_____

_____

PUPPY WEIGHT CHART

Sire _____ Dam _____ Litter DOB _____

See page 7.

Day / Pup#	10	11	12	13	14	15	16	17	18	19	20	21
1												
2												
3												
4												
5												
6												
7												
8												
9												
10												

Notes

_____
_____
_____
_____
_____
_____
_____
_____

DEWORMING & VACCINES

Sire _____ Dam _____ Litter DOB _____

Vets recommend starting deworming pups at 2–3 weeks because of roundworm eggs passed through the milk.
Pups should be vaccinated to prevent diseases. Follow the schedule recommended by your vet. See pages 11–12.

	Date Dewormed					Vaccines Vaccine #1	Vaccine #2	Vaccine #3
Date \ Pup#	week#	week#	week#	week#	week#	Date / Vaccine Name	Date / Vaccine Name	Date / Vaccine Name
1								
2								
3								
4								
5								
6								
7								
8								
9								
10								

95

PUPPY EVALUATION NOTES

Sire _____ Dam _____ Litter DOB _____

Puppy evaluation is an ongoing process that begins at birth. Use this page to record your observations about structure and temperament while pups' are standing, playing, and running free. Around 8 weeks of age a puppy is typically a mini representation of their adult silhouette. It's a wonderful opportunity to evaluate each puppy in more detail. Breed-specific and general knowledge of dogs is necessary in order to correctly evaluate your litter. Refer to the official breed standard for guidance. See page 141, Recommended Resources.

_____
_____
_____
_____
_____
_____
_____
_____
_____
_____
_____
_____
_____
_____
_____
_____
_____
_____
_____
_____
_____
_____

The whole is greater than the sum of its parts. —Aristotle

PUPPY/OWNER INFORMATION

Sire _____ Dam _____

Litter Date of Birth _____ # of males_____ # of females _____ Litter Reg # _____

Pup #1 Name _____ Litter # _____

Microchip _____Color/Markings _____

Owner(s) Name _____ Tel _____

Address _____ E-mail _____

Co-owner(s) Name _____ Tel _____

Address_____ E-mail_____

Date of Sale/Gift _____ Limited/Full Registration _____ Date Deceased _____

Pup #2 Name _____ Litter # _____

Microchip _____Color/Markings _____

Owner(s) Name _____ Tel _____

Address _____ E-mail _____

Co-owner(s) Name _____ Tel _____

Address_____ E-mail_____

Date of Sale/Gift _____ Limited/Full Registration _____ Date Deceased _____

Pup #3 Name _____ Litter # _____

Microchip _____Color/Markings _____

Owner(s) Name _____ Tel _____

Address _____ E-mail _____

Co-owner(s) Name _____ Tel _____

Address_____ E-mail_____

Date of Sale/Gift _____ Limited/Full Registration _____ Date Deceased _____

Pup #4 Name _____ Litter # _____

Microchip _____Color/Markings _____

Owner(s) Name _____ Tel _____

Address _____ E-mail _____

Co-owner(s) Name _____ Tel _____

Address_____ E-mail_____

Date of Sale/Gift _____ Limited/Full Registration _____ Date Deceased _____

Pup #5 Name _____ Litter # _____

Microchip _____Color/Markings _____

Owner(s) Name _____ Tel _____

Address _____ E-mail _____

Co-owner(s) Name _____ Tel _____

Address_____ E-mail_____

Date of Sale/Gift _____ Limited/Full Registration _____ Date Deceased _____

Properly trained, a man can be a dog's best friend. —Corey Ford

Sire _____ Dam _____

Litter Date of Birth _____ # of males _____ # of females _____ Litter Reg # _____

Pup #6 Name _____ Litter # _____

Microchip _____ Color/Markings _____

Owner(s) Name _____ Tel _____

Address _____ E-mail _____

Co-owner(s) Name _____ Tel _____

Address _____ E-mail _____

Date of Sale/Gift _____ Limited/Full Registration _____ Date Deceased _____

Pup #7 Name _____ Litter # _____

Microchip _____ Color/Markings _____

Owner(s) Name _____ Tel _____

Address _____ E-mail _____

Co-owner(s) Name _____ Tel _____

Address _____ E-mail _____

Date of Sale/Gift _____ Limited/Full Registration _____ Date Deceased _____

Pup #8 Name _____ Litter # _____

Microchip _____ Color/Markings _____

Owner(s) Name _____ Tel _____

Address _____ E-mail _____

Co-owner(s) Name _____ Tel _____

Address _____ E-mail _____

Date of Sale/Gift _____ Limited/Full Registration _____ Date Deceased _____

Pup #9 Name _____ Litter # _____

Microchip _____ Color/Markings _____

Owner(s) Name _____ Tel _____

Address _____ E-mail _____

Co-owner(s) Name _____ Tel _____

Address _____ E-mail _____

Date of Sale/Gift _____ Limited/Full Registration _____ Date Deceased _____

Pup #10 Name _____ Litter # _____

Microchip _____ Color/Markings _____

Owner(s) Name _____ Tel _____

Address _____ E-mail _____

Co-owner(s) Name _____ Tel _____

Address _____ E-mail _____

Date of Sale/Gift _____ Limited/Full Registration _____ Date Deceased _____

PHOTO MEMORY OF A PRECIOUS LITTER

Sire _____ Dam _____ Litter DOB _____

DAM INFORMATION

Name _____ DOB _____

AKC# _____ Other registry # _____

Breed _____ Color/Markings _____

DNA# _____ Microchip# _____

Owner(s) Name _____ Telephone _____

Address _____ E-mail _____

Breeder(s)Name _____ Telephone _____

Address _____ E-mail _____

Date of Acquisition _____ Date & Duration of Lease, if any _____

Health Tests completed (i.e., OFA, CERF) _____

_____

_____

_____

_____

SIRE INFORMATION

Name _____ DOB _____

AKC# _____ Other registry # _____

Breed _____ Color/Markings _____

DNA# _____ Microchip# _____

Owner(s) Name _____ Telephone _____

Address _____ E-mail _____

Breeder(s)Name _____ Telephone _____

Address _____ E-mail _____

Date of Acquisition _____

Health Tests completed (i.e., OFA, CERF) _____

_____

_____

_____

_____

PREPARING FOR WHELP

Sire_____ Dam_____

Breeding Dates: _____ Natural/AI _____

Place of Mating _____ Persons Handling the Mating _____

Ultrasound/Radiograph results:_____ Due Date: _____

Fecal test results: _____

Monitor Dam's Temperature a week prior to whelp—see page 6

DATE:_____Temp AM _____Temp Midday _____Temp PM_____Temp Nighttime _____

DATE:_____Temp AM _____Temp Midday _____Temp PM_____Temp Nighttime _____

DATE:_____Temp AM _____Temp Midday _____Temp PM_____Temp Nighttime _____

DATE:_____Temp AM _____Temp Midday _____Temp PM_____Temp Nighttime _____

DATE:_____Temp AM _____Temp Midday _____Temp PM_____Temp Nighttime _____

DATE:_____Temp AM _____Temp Midday _____Temp PM_____Temp Nighttime _____

DATE:_____Temp AM _____Temp Midday _____Temp PM_____Temp Nighttime _____

WARNING! Some mothers-to-be may not show a temperature drop or give prior warning before giving birth. In the week preceding her due date it is strongly advised not to leave her unattended day or night.

Notes _____
_____
_____

Watch for temperature drop to 99ºF or below, or 2 degrees below her normal temperature.

_____
_____
_____

THE PUPS HAVE ARRIVED!

Sire_____ Dam_____

Hard labor begins _____ Water bag appears _____ Litter DOB _____

Refer to pages 6–7 for signs of impending whelp and stages of labor. Also Recommended Resources, page 141.

Puppy #	Time	Sex	Weight	Afterbirth?	Status	Color/Markings
1						
2						
3						
4						
5						
6						
7						
8						
9						
10						

Additional Notes

_____

_____

_____

_____

_____

_____

PUPPY WEIGHT CHART

Sire _____ Dam _____ Litter DOB _____

It is recommended to weigh your pups twice daily for the first week. See page 7.

Day / Pup#	1		2		3		4		5		6		7		8	9
	am	pm	am	pm	am	pm	am	pm	am	pm	am	pm	am	pm		
1																
2	am	pm	am	pm	am	pm	am	pm	am	pm	am	pm	am	pm		
3	am	pm	am	pm	am	pm	am	pm	am	pm	am	pm	am	pm		
4	am	pm	am	pm	am	pm	am	pm	am	pm	am	pm	am	pm		
5	am	pm	am	pm	am	pm	am	pm	am	pm	am	pm	am	pm		
6	am	pm	am	pm	am	pm	am	pm	am	pm	am	pm	am	pm		
7	am	pm	am	pm	am	pm	am	pm	am	pm	am	pm	am	pm		
8	am	pm	am	pm	am	pm	am	pm	am	pm	am	pm	am	pm		
9	am	pm	am	pm	am	pm	am	pm	am	pm	am	pm	am	pm		
10	am	pm	am	pm	am	pm	am	pm	am	pm	am	pm	am	pm		

Notes

_____

_____

_____

_____

_____

_____

_____

PUPPY WEIGHT CHART

Sire _____ Dam _____ Litter DOB _____

See page 7.

Day / Pup#	10	11	12	13	14	15	16	17	18	19	20	21
1												
2												
3												
4												
5												
6												
7												
8												
9												
10												

Notes

_____
_____
_____
_____
_____
_____
_____

DEWORMING & VACCINES

Sire _____ Dam _____ Litter DOB _____

Vets recommend starting deworming pups at 2–3 weeks because of roundworm eggs passed through the milk.
Pups should be vaccinated to prevent diseases. Follow the schedule recommended by your vet. See pages 11–12.

	Date Dewormed					Vaccines Vaccine #1	Vaccine #2	Vaccine #3
Date / Pup#	week#	week#	week#	week#	week#	Vaccine Name / Date	Vaccine Name / Date	Vaccine Name / Date
1								
2								
3								
4								
5								
6								
7								
8								
9								
10								

PUPPY EVALUATION NOTES

Sire _____ Dam _____ Litter DOB _____

Puppy evaluation is an ongoing process that begins at birth. Use this page to record your observations about structure and temperament while pups' are standing, playing, and running free. Around 8 weeks of age a puppy is typically a mini representation of their adult silhouette. It's a wonderful opportunity to evaluate each puppy in more detail. Breed-specific and general knowledge of dogs is necessary in order to correctly evaluate your litter. Refer to the official breed standard for guidance. See page 141, Recommended Resources.

_____
_____
_____
_____
_____
_____
_____
_____
_____
_____
_____
_____
_____
_____
_____
_____
_____
_____
_____
_____
_____
_____

The whole is greater than the sum of its parts. —Aristotle

PUPPY/OWNER INFORMATION

Sire _____ Dam _____

Litter Date of Birth _____ # of males _____ # of females _____ Litter Reg # _____

Pup #1 Name _____ Litter # _____

Microchip _____ Color/Markings _____

Owner(s) Name _____ Tel _____

Address _____ E-mail _____

Co-owner(s) Name _____ Tel _____

Address _____ E-mail _____

Date of Sale/Gift _____ Limited/Full Registration _____ Date Deceased _____

Pup #2 Name _____ Litter # _____

Microchip _____ Color/Markings _____

Owner(s) Name _____ Tel _____

Address _____ E-mail _____

Co-owner(s) Name _____ Tel _____

Address _____ E-mail _____

Date of Sale/Gift _____ Limited/Full Registration _____ Date Deceased _____

Pup #3 Name _____ Litter # _____

Microchip _____ Color/Markings _____

Owner(s) Name _____ Tel _____

Address _____ E-mail _____

Co-owner(s) Name _____ Tel _____

Address _____ E-mail _____

Date of Sale/Gift _____ Limited/Full Registration _____ Date Deceased _____

Pup #4 Name _____ Litter # _____

Microchip _____ Color/Markings _____

Owner(s) Name _____ Tel _____

Address _____ E-mail _____

Co-owner(s) Name _____ Tel _____

Address _____ E-mail _____

Date of Sale/Gift _____ Limited/Full Registration _____ Date Deceased _____

Pup #5 Name _____ Litter # _____

Microchip _____ Color/Markings _____

Owner(s) Name _____ Tel _____

Address _____ E-mail _____

Co-owner(s) Name _____ Tel _____

Address _____ E-mail _____

Date of Sale/Gift _____ Limited/Full Registration _____ Date Deceased _____

Properly trained, a man can be a dog's best friend. —Corey Ford

Sire _____ Dam _____

Litter Date of Birth _____ # of males _____ # of females _____ Litter Reg # _____

Pup #6 Name _____ Litter # _____

Microchip _____ Color/Markings _____

Owner(s) Name _____ Tel _____

Address _____ E-mail _____

Co-owner(s) Name _____ Tel _____

Address _____ E-mail _____

Date of Sale/Gift _____ Limited/Full Registration _____ Date Deceased _____

Pup #7 Name _____ Litter # _____

Microchip _____ Color/Markings _____

Owner(s) Name _____ Tel _____

Address _____ E-mail _____

Co-owner(s) Name _____ Tel _____

Address _____ E-mail _____

Date of Sale/Gift _____ Limited/Full Registration _____ Date Deceased _____

Pup #8 Name _____ Litter # _____

Microchip _____ Color/Markings _____

Owner(s) Name _____ Tel _____

Address _____ E-mail _____

Co-owner(s) Name _____ Tel _____

Address _____ E-mail _____

Date of Sale/Gift _____ Limited/Full Registration _____ Date Deceased _____

Pup #9 Name _____ Litter # _____

Microchip _____ Color/Markings _____

Owner(s) Name _____ Tel _____

Address _____ E-mail _____

Co-owner(s) Name _____ Tel _____

Address _____ E-mail _____

Date of Sale/Gift _____ Limited/Full Registration _____ Date Deceased _____

Pup #10 Name _____ Litter # _____

Microchip _____ Color/Markings _____

Owner(s) Name _____ Tel _____

Address _____ E-mail _____

Co-owner(s) Name _____ Tel _____

Address _____ E-mail _____

Date of Sale/Gift _____ Limited/Full Registration _____ Date Deceased _____

PHOTO MEMORY OF A PRECIOUS LITTER

Sire _____ Dam _____ Litter DOB _____

DAM INFORMATION

Name _____ DOB _____

AKC# _____ Other registry # _____

Breed _____ Color/Markings _____

DNA# _____ Microchip# _____

Owner(s) Name _____ Telephone _____

Address _____ E-mail _____

Breeder(s)Name _____ Telephone _____

Address _____ E-mail _____

Date of Acquisition _____ Date & Duration of Lease, if any _____

Health Tests completed (i.e., OFA, CERF) _____

_____

_____

_____

_____

SIRE INFORMATION

Name _____ DOB _____

AKC# _____ Other registry # _____

Breed _____ Color/Markings _____

DNA# _____ Microchip# _____

Owner(s) Name _____ Telephone _____

Address _____ E-mail _____

Breeder(s)Name _____ Telephone _____

Address _____ E-mail _____

Date of Acquisition _____

Health Tests completed (i.e., OFA, CERF) _____

_____

_____

_____

_____

PREPARING FOR WHELP

Sire_____ Dam_____

Breeding Dates: _____ Natural/AI _____

Place of Mating _____ Persons Handling the Mating _____

Ultrasound/Radiograph results:_____ Due Date: _____

Fecal test results: _____

Monitor Dam's Temperature a week prior to whelp—see page 6

DATE:_____Temp AM _____Temp Midday _____Temp PM_____Temp Nighttime _____

DATE:_____Temp AM _____Temp Midday _____Temp PM_____Temp Nighttime _____

DATE:_____Temp AM _____Temp Midday _____Temp PM_____Temp Nighttime _____

DATE:_____Temp AM _____Temp Midday _____Temp PM_____Temp Nighttime _____

DATE:_____Temp AM _____Temp Midday _____Temp PM_____Temp Nighttime _____

DATE:_____Temp AM _____Temp Midday _____Temp PM_____Temp Nighttime _____

DATE:_____Temp AM _____Temp Midday _____Temp PM_____Temp Nighttime _____

WARNING! Some mothers-to-be may not show a temperature drop or give prior warning before giving birth. In the week preceding her due date it is strongly advised not to leave her unattended day or night.

Notes _____

_____

_____

_____

_____

_____

Watch for temperature drop to 99ºF or below, or 2 degrees below her normal temperature.

THE PUPS HAVE ARRIVED!

Sire_____ Dam_____

Hard labor begins _____ Water bag appears _____ Litter DOB _____

Refer to pages 6–7 for signs of impending whelp and stages of labor. Also Recommended Resources, page 141.

Puppy #	Time	Sex	Weight	Afterbirth?	Status	Color/Markings
1						
2						
3						
4						
5						
6						
7						
8						
9						
10						

Additional Notes

_____

_____

_____

_____

_____

_____

PUPPY WEIGHT CHART

Sire _____ Dam _____ Litter DOB _____

It is recommended to weigh your pups twice daily for the first week. See page 7.

Day / Pup#	1		2		3		4		5		6		7		8	9
	am	pm	am	pm	am	pm	am	pm	am	pm	am	pm	am	pm		
1																
2	am	pm	am	pm	am	pm	am	pm	am	pm	am	pm	am	pm		
3	am	pm	am	pm	am	pm	am	pm	am	pm	am	pm	am	pm		
4	am	pm	am	pm	am	pm	am	pm	am	pm	am	pm	am	pm		
5	am	pm	am	pm	am	pm	am	pm	am	pm	am	pm	am	pm		
6	am	pm	am	pm	am	pm	am	pm	am	pm	am	pm	am	pm		
7	am	pm	am	pm	am	pm	am	pm	am	pm	am	pm	am	pm		
8	am	pm	am	pm	am	pm	am	pm	am	pm	am	pm	am	pm		
9	am	pm	am	pm	am	pm	am	pm	am	pm	am	pm	am	pm		
10	am	pm	am	pm	am	pm	am	pm	am	pm	am	pm	am	pm		

Notes

PUPPY WEIGHT CHART

Sire _____ Dam _____ Litter DOB _____

See page 7.

Day / Pup#	10	11	12	13	14	15	16	17	18	19	20	21
1												
2												
3												
4												
5												
6												
7												
8												
9												
10												

Notes

_____
_____
_____
_____
_____
_____
_____
_____

114

DEWORMING & VACCINES

Sire _____ Dam _____ Litter DOB _____

Vets recommend starting deworming pups at 2–3 weeks because of roundworm eggs passed through the milk.
Pups should be vaccinated to prevent diseases. Follow the schedule recommended by your vet. See pages 11–12.

Date Dewormed / Vaccines

Date \ Pup#	week#	week#	week#	week#	week#	Vaccine #1 — Vaccine Name / Date	Vaccine #2 — Vaccine Name / Date	Vaccine #3 — Vaccine Name / Date
1								
2								
3								
4								
5								
6								
7								
8								
9								
10								

PUPPY EVALUATION NOTES

Sire _____ Dam _____ Litter DOB _____

Puppy evaluation is an ongoing process that begins at birth. Use this page to record your observations about structure and temperament while pups' are standing, playing, and running free. Around 8 weeks of age a puppy is typically a mini representation of their adult silhouette. It's a wonderful opportunity to evaluate each puppy in more detail. Breed-specific and general knowledge of dogs is necessary in order to correctly evaluate your litter. Refer to the official breed standard for guidance. See page 141, Recommended Resources.

_____

_____

_____

_____

_____

_____

_____

_____

_____

_____

_____

_____

_____

_____

_____

_____

_____

_____

_____

_____

_____

_____

_____

The whole is greater than the sum of its parts. —Aristotle

PUPPY/OWNER INFORMATION

Sire _____ Dam _____

Litter Date of Birth _____ # of males _____ # of females _____ Litter Reg # _____

Pup #1 Name _____ Litter # _____

Microchip _____ Color/Markings _____

Owner(s) Name _____ Tel _____

Address _____ E-mail _____

Co-owner(s) Name _____ Tel _____

Address _____ E-mail _____

Date of Sale/Gift _____ Limited/Full Registration _____ Date Deceased _____

Pup #2 Name _____ Litter # _____

Microchip _____ Color/Markings _____

Owner(s) Name _____ Tel _____

Address _____ E-mail _____

Co-owner(s) Name _____ Tel _____

Address _____ E-mail _____

Date of Sale/Gift _____ Limited/Full Registration _____ Date Deceased _____

Pup #3 Name _____ Litter # _____

Microchip _____ Color/Markings _____

Owner(s) Name _____ Tel _____

Address _____ E-mail _____

Co-owner(s) Name _____ Tel _____

Address _____ E-mail _____

Date of Sale/Gift _____ Limited/Full Registration _____ Date Deceased _____

Pup #4 Name _____ Litter # _____

Microchip _____ Color/Markings _____

Owner(s) Name _____ Tel _____

Address _____ E-mail _____

Co-owner(s) Name _____ Tel _____

Address _____ E-mail _____

Date of Sale/Gift _____ Limited/Full Registration _____ Date Deceased _____

Pup #5 Name _____ Litter # _____

Microchip _____ Color/Markings _____

Owner(s) Name _____ Tel _____

Address _____ E-mail _____

Co-owner(s) Name _____ Tel _____

Address _____ E-mail _____

Date of Sale/Gift _____ Limited/Full Registration _____ Date Deceased _____

Properly trained, a man can be a dog's best friend. —Corey Ford

Sire _____ Dam _____

Litter Date of Birth _____ # of males_____ # of females _____ Litter Reg # _____

Pup #6 Name _____ Litter # _____

Microchip _____ Color/Markings _____

Owner(s) Name _____ Tel _____

Address _____ E-mail _____

Co-owner(s) Name _____ Tel _____

Address_____ E-mail_____

Date of Sale/Gift _____ Limited/Full Registration _____ Date Deceased _____

Pup #7 Name _____ Litter # _____

Microchip _____ Color/Markings _____

Owner(s) Name _____ Tel _____

Address _____ E-mail _____

Co-owner(s) Name _____ Tel _____

Address_____ E-mail_____

Date of Sale/Gift _____ Limited/Full Registration _____ Date Deceased _____

Pup #8 Name _____ Litter # _____

Microchip _____ Color/Markings _____

Owner(s) Name _____ Tel _____

Address _____ E-mail _____

Co-owner(s) Name _____ Tel _____

Address_____ E-mail_____

Date of Sale/Gift _____ Limited/Full Registration _____ Date Deceased _____

Pup #9 Name _____ Litter # _____

Microchip _____ Color/Markings _____

Owner(s) Name _____ Tel _____

Address _____ E-mail _____

Co-owner(s) Name _____ Tel _____

Address_____ E-mail_____

Date of Sale/Gift _____ Limited/Full Registration _____ Date Deceased _____

Pup #10 Name _____ Litter # _____

Microchip _____ Color/Markings _____

Owner(s) Name _____ Tel _____

Address _____ E-mail _____

Co-owner(s) Name _____ Tel _____

Address_____ E-mail_____

Date of Sale/Gift _____ Limited/Full Registration _____ Date Deceased _____

PHOTO MEMORY OF A PRECIOUS LITTER

Sire _____ Dam _____ Litter DOB _____

DAM INFORMATION

Name _____ DOB _____

AKC# _____ Other registry # _____

Breed _____ Color/Markings _____

DNA# _____ Microchip# _____

Owner(s) Name _____ Telephone _____

Address _____ E-mail _____

Breeder(s)Name _____ Telephone _____

Address _____ E-mail _____

Date of Acquisition _____ Date & Duration of Lease, if any _____

Health Tests completed (i.e., OFA, CERF) _____

_____

_____

_____

_____

SIRE INFORMATION

Name _____ DOB _____

AKC# _____ Other registry # _____

Breed _____ Color/Markings _____

DNA# _____ Microchip# _____

Owner(s) Name _____ Telephone _____

Address _____ E-mail _____

Breeder(s)Name _____ Telephone _____

Address _____ E-mail _____

Date of Acquisition _____

Health Tests completed (i.e., OFA, CERF) _____

_____

_____

_____

_____

PREPARING FOR WHELP

Sire_____ Dam_____

Breeding Dates: _____ Natural/AI _____

Place of Mating _____ Persons Handling the Mating _____

Ultrasound/Radiograph results:_____ Due Date: _____

Fecal test results: _____

Monitor Dam's Temperature a week prior to whelp—see page 6

DATE:_____Temp AM _____Temp Midday _____Temp PM_____Temp Nighttime _____

DATE:_____Temp AM _____Temp Midday _____Temp PM_____Temp Nighttime _____

DATE:_____Temp AM _____Temp Midday _____Temp PM_____Temp Nighttime _____

DATE:_____Temp AM _____Temp Midday _____Temp PM_____Temp Nighttime _____

DATE:_____Temp AM _____Temp Midday _____Temp PM_____Temp Nighttime _____

DATE:_____Temp AM _____Temp Midday _____Temp PM_____Temp Nighttime _____

DATE:_____Temp AM _____Temp Midday _____Temp PM_____Temp Nighttime _____

WARNING! Some mothers-to-be may not show a temperature drop or give prior warning before giving birth. In the week preceding her due date it is strongly advised not to leave her unattended day or night.

Notes _____

_____

_____

_____

Watch for temperature drop to 99ºF or below, or 2 degrees below her normal temperature.

_____

_____

THE PUPS HAVE ARRIVED!

Sire_____ Dam_____

Hard labor begins _____ Water bag appears _____ Litter DOB _____

Refer to pages 6–7 for signs of impending whelp and stages of labor. Also Recommended Resources, page 141.

Puppy #	Time	Sex	Weight	Afterbirth?	Status	Color/Markings
1						
2						
3						
4						
5						
6						
7						
8						
9						
10						

Additional Notes
_____
_____
_____
_____
_____

122

PUPPY WEIGHT CHART

Sire _____ Dam _____ Litter DOB _____

It is recommended to weigh your pups twice daily for the first week. See page 7.

Pup# \ Day	1 am	1 pm	2 am	2 pm	3 am	3 pm	4 am	4 pm	5 am	5 pm	6 am	6 pm	7 am	7 pm	8	9
1																
2																
3																
4																
5																
6																
7																
8																
9																
10																

Notes

_____

_____

_____

_____

_____

_____

_____

PUPPY WEIGHT CHART

Sire _____ Dam _____ Litter DOB _____

See page 7.

Day / Pup#	10	11	12	13	14	15	16	17	18	19	20	21
1												
2												
3												
4												
5												
6												
7												
8												
9												
10												

Notes

_____

_____

_____

_____

_____

_____

_____

DEWORMING & VACCINES

Sire _____ Dam _____ Litter DOB _____

Vets recommend starting deworming pups at 2–3 weeks because of roundworm eggs passed through the milk.
Pups should be vaccinated to prevent diseases. Follow the schedule recommended by your vet. See pages 11–12.

Date Dewormed / Vaccines

Date / Pup#	week#	week#	week#	week#	week#	Vaccine #1 — Vaccine Name / Date	Vaccine #2 — Vaccine Name / Date	Vaccine #3 — Vaccine Name / Date
1								
2								
3								
4								
5								
6								
7								
8								
9								
10								

PUPPY EVALUATION NOTES

Sire _____ Dam _____ Litter DOB _____

Puppy evaluation is an ongoing process that begins at birth. Use this page to record your observations about structure and temperament while pups' are standing, playing, and running free. Around 8 weeks of age a puppy is typically a mini representation of their adult silhouette. It's a wonderful opportunity to evaluate each puppy in more detail. Breed-specific and general knowledge of dogs is necessary in order to correctly evaluate your litter. Refer to the official breed standard for guidance. See page 141, Recommended Resources.

_____
_____
_____
_____
_____
_____
_____
_____
_____
_____
_____
_____
_____
_____
_____
_____
_____
_____
_____
_____
_____
_____
_____

The whole is greater than the sum of its parts. —Aristotle

PUPPY/OWNER INFORMATION

Sire _____ Dam _____

Litter Date of Birth _____ # of males _____ # of females _____ Litter Reg # _____

Pup #1 Name _____ Litter # _____

Microchip _____ Color/Markings _____

Owner(s) Name _____ Tel _____

Address _____ E-mail _____

Co-owner(s) Name _____ Tel _____

Address _____ E-mail _____

Date of Sale/Gift _____ Limited/Full Registration _____ Date Deceased _____

Pup #2 Name _____ Litter # _____

Microchip _____ Color/Markings _____

Owner(s) Name _____ Tel _____

Address _____ E-mail _____

Co-owner(s) Name _____ Tel _____

Address _____ E-mail _____

Date of Sale/Gift _____ Limited/Full Registration _____ Date Deceased _____

Pup #3 Name _____ Litter # _____

Microchip _____ Color/Markings _____

Owner(s) Name _____ Tel _____

Address _____ E-mail _____

Co-owner(s) Name _____ Tel _____

Address _____ E-mail _____

Date of Sale/Gift _____ Limited/Full Registration _____ Date Deceased _____

Pup #4 Name _____ Litter # _____

Microchip _____ Color/Markings _____

Owner(s) Name _____ Tel _____

Address _____ E-mail _____

Co-owner(s) Name _____ Tel _____

Address _____ E-mail _____

Date of Sale/Gift _____ Limited/Full Registration _____ Date Deceased _____

Pup #5 Name _____ Litter # _____

Microchip _____ Color/Markings _____

Owner(s) Name _____ Tel _____

Address _____ E-mail _____

Co-owner(s) Name _____ Tel _____

Address _____ E-mail _____

Date of Sale/Gift _____ Limited/Full Registration _____ Date Deceased _____

Properly trained, a man can be a dog's best friend. —Corey Ford

Sire _____ Dam _____

Litter Date of Birth _____ # of males_____ # of females _____ Litter Reg # _____

Pup #6 Name _____ Litter # _____

Microchip _____ Color/Markings _____

Owner(s) Name _____ Tel _____

Address _____ E-mail _____

Co-owner(s) Name _____ Tel _____

Address_____ E-mail_____

Date of Sale/Gift _____ Limited/Full Registration _____ Date Deceased _____

Pup #7 Name _____ Litter # _____

Microchip _____ Color/Markings _____

Owner(s) Name _____ Tel _____

Address _____ E-mail _____

Co-owner(s) Name _____ Tel _____

Address_____ E-mail_____

Date of Sale/Gift _____ Limited/Full Registration _____ Date Deceased _____

Pup #8 Name _____ Litter # _____

Microchip _____ Color/Markings _____

Owner(s) Name _____ Tel _____

Address _____ E-mail _____

Co-owner(s) Name _____ Tel _____

Address_____ E-mail_____

Date of Sale/Gift _____ Limited/Full Registration _____ Date Deceased _____

Pup #9 Name _____ Litter # _____

Microchip _____ Color/Markings _____

Owner(s) Name _____ Tel _____

Address _____ E-mail _____

Co-owner(s) Name _____ Tel _____

Address_____ E-mail_____

Date of Sale/Gift _____ Limited/Full Registration _____ Date Deceased _____

Pup #10 Name _____ Litter # _____

Microchip _____ Color/Markings _____

Owner(s) Name _____ Tel _____

Address _____ E-mail _____

Co-owner(s) Name _____ Tel _____

Address_____ E-mail_____

Date of Sale/Gift _____ Limited/Full Registration _____ Date Deceased _____

PHOTO MEMORY OF A PRECIOUS LITTER

Sire _____ Dam _____ Litter DOB _____

DAM INFORMATION

Name _____ DOB _____

AKC# _____ Other registry # _____

Breed _____ Color/Markings _____

DNA# _____ Microchip# _____

Owner(s) Name _____ Telephone _____

Address _____ E-mail _____

Breeder(s)Name _____ Telephone _____

Address _____ E-mail _____

Date of Acquisition _____ Date & Duration of Lease, if any _____

Health Tests completed (i.e., OFA, CERF) _____

_____

_____

_____

_____

SIRE INFORMATION

Name _____ DOB _____

AKC# _____ Other registry # _____

Breed _____ Color/Markings _____

DNA# _____ Microchip# _____

Owner(s) Name _____ Telephone _____

Address _____ E-mail _____

Breeder(s)Name _____ Telephone _____

Address _____ E-mail _____

Date of Acquisition _____

Health Tests completed (i.e., OFA, CERF) _____

_____

_____

_____

_____

PREPARING FOR WHELP

Sire_____ Dam_____

Breeding Dates: _____ Natural/AI _____

Place of Mating _____ Persons Handling the Mating _____

Ultrasound/Radiograph results:_____ Due Date: _____

Fecal test results: _____

Monitor Dam's Temperature a week prior to whelp—see page 6

DATE:_____Temp AM _____Temp Midday _____Temp PM_____Temp Nighttime _____

DATE:_____Temp AM _____Temp Midday _____Temp PM_____Temp Nighttime _____

DATE:_____Temp AM _____Temp Midday _____Temp PM_____Temp Nighttime _____

DATE:_____Temp AM _____Temp Midday _____Temp PM_____Temp Nighttime _____

DATE:_____Temp AM _____Temp Midday _____Temp PM_____Temp Nighttime _____

DATE:_____Temp AM _____Temp Midday _____Temp PM_____Temp Nighttime _____

DATE:_____Temp AM _____Temp Midday _____Temp PM_____Temp Nighttime _____

WARNING! Some mothers-to-be may not show a temperature drop or give prior warning before giving birth. In the week preceding her due date it is strongly advised not to leave her unattended day or night.

Notes _____

_____

_____

_____

Watch for temperature drop to 99ºF or below, or 2 degrees below her normal temperature.

_____

_____

131

THE PUPS HAVE ARRIVED!

Sire_____ Dam_____

Hard labor begins _____ Water bag appears _____ Litter DOB _____

Refer to pages 6–7 for signs of impending whelp and stages of labor. Also Recommended Resources, page 141.

Puppy #	Time	Sex	Weight	Afterbirth?	Status	Color/Markings
1						
2						
3						
4						
5						
6						
7						
8						
9						
10						

Additional Notes
_____
_____
_____
_____
_____
_____

PUPPY WEIGHT CHART

Sire _____ Dam _____ Litter DOB _____

It is recommended to weigh your pups twice daily for the first week. See page 7.

Day Pup#	1		2		3		4		5		6		7		8	9
1	am	pm	am	pm	am	pm	am	pm	am	pm	am	pm	am	pm		
2	am	pm	am	pm	am	pm	am	pm	am	pm	am	pm	am	pm		
3	am	pm	am	pm	am	pm	am	pm	am	pm	am	pm	am	pm		
4	am	pm	am	pm	am	pm	am	pm	am	pm	am	pm	am	pm		
5	am	pm	am	pm	am	pm	am	pm	am	pm	am	pm	am	pm		
6	am	pm	am	pm	am	pm	am	pm	am	pm	am	pm	am	pm		
7	am	pm	am	pm	am	pm	am	pm	am	pm	am	pm	am	pm		
8	am	pm	am	pm	am	pm	am	pm	am	pm	am	pm	am	pm		
9	am	pm	am	pm	am	pm	am	pm	am	pm	am	pm	am	pm		
10	am	pm	am	pm	am	pm	am	pm	am	pm	am	pm	am	pm		

Notes
_____
_____
_____
_____
_____
_____
_____

PUPPY WEIGHT CHART

Sire _____ Dam _____ Litter DOB _____

See page 7.

Day Pup#	10	11	12	13	14	15	16	17	18	19	20	21
1												
2												
3												
4												
5												
6												
7												
8												
9												
10												

Notes
_____
_____
_____
_____
_____
_____
_____

DEWORMING & VACCINES

Sire _____ Dam _____ Litter DOB _____

Vets recommend starting deworming pups at 2–3 weeks because of roundworm eggs passed through the milk.
Pups should be vaccinated to prevent diseases. Follow the schedule recommended by your vet. See pages 11–12.

Date Dewormed   Vaccines

Date / Pup#	week#	week#	week#	week#	week#	Vaccine #1 Vaccine Name / Date	Vaccine #2 Vaccine Name / Date	Vaccine #3 Vaccine Name / Date
1								
2								
3								
4								
5								
6								
7								
8								
9								
10								

PUPPY EVALUATION NOTES

Sire _____ Dam _____ Litter DOB _____

Puppy evaluation is an ongoing process that begins at birth. Use this page to record your observations about structure and temperament while pups' are standing, playing, and running free. Around 8 weeks of age a puppy is typically a mini representation of their adult silhouette. It's a wonderful opportunity to evaluate each puppy in more detail. Breed-specific and general knowledge of dogs is necessary in order to correctly evaluate your litter. Refer to the official breed standard for guidance. See page 141, Recommended Resources.

_____

_____

_____

_____

_____

_____

_____

_____

_____

_____

_____

_____

_____

_____

_____

_____

_____

_____

_____

_____

_____

_____

_____

_____

The whole is greater than the sum of its parts. —Aristotle

PUPPY/OWNER INFORMATION

Sire _____ Dam _____

Litter Date of Birth _____ # of males_____ # of females _____ Litter Reg # _____

Pup #1 Name _____ Litter # _____

Microchip _____Color/Markings _____

Owner(s) Name _____ Tel _____

Address _____ E-mail _____

Co-owner(s) Name _____ Tel _____

Address _____ E-mail _____

Date of Sale/Gift _____ Limited/Full Registration _____ Date Deceased _____

Pup #2 Name _____ Litter # _____

Microchip _____Color/Markings _____

Owner(s) Name _____ Tel _____

Address _____ E-mail _____

Co-owner(s) Name _____ Tel _____

Address _____ E-mail _____

Date of Sale/Gift _____ Limited/Full Registration _____ Date Deceased _____

Pup #3 Name _____ Litter # _____

Microchip _____Color/Markings _____

Owner(s) Name _____ Tel _____

Address _____ E-mail _____

Co-owner(s) Name _____ Tel _____

Address _____ E-mail _____

Date of Sale/Gift _____ Limited/Full Registration _____ Date Deceased _____

Pup #4 Name _____ Litter # _____

Microchip _____Color/Markings _____

Owner(s) Name _____ Tel _____

Address _____ E-mail _____

Co-owner(s) Name _____ Tel _____

Address _____ E-mail _____

Date of Sale/Gift _____ Limited/Full Registration _____ Date Deceased _____

Pup #5 Name _____ Litter # _____

Microchip _____Color/Markings _____

Owner(s) Name _____ Tel _____

Address _____ E-mail _____

Co-owner(s) Name _____ Tel _____

Address _____ E-mail _____

Date of Sale/Gift _____ Limited/Full Registration _____ Date Deceased _____

Sire _____ Dam _____

Litter Date of Birth _____ # of males _____ # of females _____ Litter Reg # _____

Pup #6 Name _____ Litter # _____

Microchip _____ Color/Markings _____

Owner(s) Name _____ Tel _____

Address _____ E-mail _____

Co-owner(s) Name _____ Tel _____

Address _____ E-mail _____

Date of Sale/Gift _____ Limited/Full Registration _____ Date Deceased _____

Pup #7 Name _____ Litter # _____

Microchip _____ Color/Markings _____

Owner(s) Name _____ Tel _____

Address _____ E-mail _____

Co-owner(s) Name _____ Tel _____

Address _____ E-mail _____

Date of Sale/Gift _____ Limited/Full Registration _____ Date Deceased _____

Pup #8 Name _____ Litter # _____

Microchip _____ Color/Markings _____

Owner(s) Name _____ Tel _____

Address _____ E-mail _____

Co-owner(s) Name _____ Tel _____

Address _____ E-mail _____

Date of Sale/Gift _____ Limited/Full Registration _____ Date Deceased _____

Pup #9 Name _____ Litter # _____

Microchip _____ Color/Markings _____

Owner(s) Name _____ Tel _____

Address _____ E-mail _____

Co-owner(s) Name _____ Tel _____

Address _____ E-mail _____

Date of Sale/Gift _____ Limited/Full Registration _____ Date Deceased _____

Pup #10 Name _____ Litter # _____

Microchip _____ Color/Markings _____

Owner(s) Name _____ Tel _____

Address _____ E-mail _____

Co-owner(s) Name _____ Tel _____

Address _____ E-mail _____

Date of Sale/Gift _____ Limited/Full Registration _____ Date Deceased _____

IS BREEDING AN ART?

In pondering the topic of breeding as an art, I was pleasantly surprised to find one of the most famous artists of all time compared to a breeder! In her book "Born to Win," Patricia Craig Trotter says, "Leonardo da Vinci would have made a good breeder—he was curious, creative, dedicated, and eternally fascinated with his work." Does that sound like you? Are you curious, dedicated, and fascinated by your work as a breeder? Maybe you're an artist and didn't even know it!

What exactly is "Art"? The first and broadest definition of the word "art" comes from the older Latin meaning which translates: a "skill" or "craft." "Britannica Online" defines art as "the use of skill and imagination in the creation of aesthetic objects, environments, or experiences that can be shared with others." Breeding definitely requires many skills. "Skill" is the ability to use one's knowledge to do something well. "Imagination" comes in when a breeder is creative and resourceful with those skills in order to achieve his goals. Ideally, breeding combines both skill and imagination (creativity) in the pursuit to breed better dogs. That is when breeding becomes an art!

Breeders actually have much in common with Leonardo da Vinci. We are hard-working, curious, creative, dedicated to our dogs, and fascinated by our work. Breeding becomes our art as we strive for excellence and that all-illusive goal of perfection described in each breed standard. We are prepared to make sacrifices in the hopes of creating a work that will endure for generations to come. Like da Vinci, who was a painter, sculptor, inventor, and draftsman, we also wear many hats and thirst for knowledge in almost every area related to dogs: whelping and raising puppies, evaluating and picking puppies, conditioning and nutrition, health, genetics, training, and even the delicate art of placing pups in the

Where the spirit does not work with the hand, there is no art.
—Leonardo da Vinci

right homes. We are also educators and the advocates for our breed—we seek to protect it in every sense of the word. When I made the first strokes on my canvas, I certainly didn't know all these things and there were definitely a few tears mixed among the paint. All breeders experience heart-wrenching moments—health issues, whelping issues, dreams that fall to pieces—and wonder, what on earth did I paint? It made sense when I began, and now it appears to be a chaotic, colorful mess! All art takes courage. Take heart, even Leonardo experienced moments of humiliation and defeat. Ask questions, continue learning, consult other breeders and mentors, and never forget to listen to your inner voice—the creative artistic core that is uniquely yours. It is often in those quiet moments that we dip our paint brush deep into our soul, reflect on our failures, and find new and better ways to express our art.

In studying Leonardo's great achievements, it is worth noting he also had a humble beginning and mentors to inspire his path. Having a trusted mentor(s) is definitely an asset for any aspiring breeder. The mentor shares knowledge, guides, inspires, and helps his mentee hone his skills. However it's not so easy to mentor "imagination." Imagination (creativity) is very personal: the way we plan and implement ideas into a breeding program, how we select a sire, profile a pedigree, or choose to inbreed, line breed or outcross to come as close as possible to the breed standard—it's what makes each breeder unique. A mentor may impart knowledge and help us discover our wings, but it is up to us to fly! Keep in mind however that the journey is long, and there are no shortcuts to creating a masterpiece. Even Leonardo did not achieve his dreams overnight!

A breeding program is a "work in progress." It is interesting to note that da Vinci's most famous work, the "Mona Lisa," was forever a work in progress and remained with him until the end of his life. It now hangs in the Louvre museum in France as a priceless national treasure for all to enjoy! Isn't that what art is all about—creating a masterpiece for our own personal enjoyment as breeders and for the enjoyment of others? Choose carefully the dogs you wish to breed, always aiming for excellence and the breed standard. Then be patient, passionate, and persistent until your dreams come true!

Breeding pure-bred dogs is truly an art. Embrace your art, shape it, protect it, and watch it reveal itself. What an awesome privilege to collaborate with nature, as "artist," in the process of creating a living, breathing work of art. While not everyone will master his art, we all have the potential to create something beautiful with the tools and colors we've been given. Let's continue to cultivate our skills and release our imagination in a combined effort to protect and enhance the pure-bred dog.

To novice and established breeders alike, I hope this record keeping book will be a treasured companion as you look back over the years at the litters you've bred. I wish you much success in your breeding programs, healthy happy pups, and a lifetime of joy at the side of your beloved canine companions!

Blessings,

Leila Grandemange

PHONE/ADDRESS BOOK

Veterinary Specialists, Pet Sitters, and Emergency Contacts

Name _____

Telephone _____ E-mail _____

Address _____

Name _____

Telephone _____ E-mail _____

Address _____

Name _____

Telephone _____ E-mail _____

Address _____

Name _____

Telephone _____ E-mail _____

Address _____

Name _____

Telephone _____ E-mail _____

Address _____

Name _____

Telephone _____ E-mail _____

Address _____

Online Shopping Sites:

_____

_____

_____

_____

_____

> Breeders must be constantly dedicated and rededicated to the fact that the most important thing a dog can be is man's best friend.
> — Patricia Craige Trotter

RECOMMENDED RESOURCES

DOG BREEDING, WHELPING, AND PUPPY CARE

Born To Win: Breed To Succeed (second edition), by Patricia Craige Trotter

Canine Reproduction and Whelping, A Dog Breeder's Guide, by Myra Savant-Harris, RN

Puppy Intensive Care—A Breeder's Guide to Care of Newborn Puppies, by Myra Savant-Harris, RN

Canine Reproduction: The Breeder's Guide, by Phyllis A. Holst

The Book of the Bitch, by J.M. Evans and Kay White (published by Henderson, 1988)

Dog Breeding, Whelping and Puppy Care, by Gary England (published by Wiley-Blackwell, 2013)

The Cavalier King Charles Spaniel in Fact and Fancy, by Barbara Garnett Wilson

Another Piece of the Puzzle: Puppy Development by Pat Hastings and Erin Ann Rouse

The Complete Dog Book, 20th Edition, by the American Kennel Club

Web Articles

- "Getting Started as a Responsible Breeder," the American Kennel Club: https://www.akc.org/breeders/resp_breeding/Articles/breeder.cfm

- "A Guide To Breeding Your Dog," the American Kennel Club: http://www.akc.org/dog-breeders/learn/guide-to-breeding/

- "Seven Foundations of a Successful Dog Breeder" by Jonathan Jeffrey Kimes: http://jonkimes.com/7Foundations.html

- The American Kennel Club Canine Health Foundation http://www.akcchf.org/canine-health/resources/

- The World Small Animal Veterinary Association • www.wsava.org UK Kennel Club Guidelines for Vaccinations can be found here

- Whelpwise • www.whelpwise.com Whelping supplies and resources

ORDER INFORMATION

Please visit
www.SunnyvillePublishing.com

Special Thanks
Sincere thanks to the veterinarians and to the long time breeder friends who shared their expertise while I was writing this book; ED&M Design; my precious family; and of course God, who makes all things possible!

CPSIA information can be obtained at www.ICGtesting.com
Printed in the USA
BVOW03*0907030615

402763BV00015B/52/P

9 780982 685457